The Authentic Pastor

GENE E. BARTLETT

Judson Press ® Valley Forge

THE AUTHENTIC PASTOR

Copyright © 1978
Judson Press, Valley Forge, PA 19481

Unless otherwise indicated, Bible quotations in this volume are in accordance with the Revised Standard Version of the Bible, copyrighted 1946, 1952 ©1971, 1973 by the Division of Christian Education of the National Council of the Churches of Christ in the U.S.A., and are used by permission.

Also quoted in this volume: *The Holy Bible,* King James Version.

Library of Congress Cataloging in Publication Data

Bartlett, Gene E.
  The authentic pastor.

  Includes bibliographical references.
  1. Pastoral theology. I. Title.
BV4011.B372   253.2   78-2523
ISBN 0-8170-0777-6

The name JUDSON PRESS is registered as a trademark in the U.S. Patent Office. Printed in the U.S.A. ✪

Introduction

We have a phrase which on occasion brings one kind of inquiry to focus. We ask of someone whom we're trying to understand: Is he for real?

The evidences are sufficient and convincing that the phrase is being directed today toward pastors. Are they for real? What in the world do they do? Since many people find life quite sufficient without anything the pastor has to offer, isn't the calling itself a vestigial organ in the social body?

There are times and conditions in the lives of most ministers when we even ask it of ourselves. Are our claims really audacious or are they simply preposterous? Often we don't feel the way we should feel if we are what we claim to be! We discover that ordination is not inoculation. We suffer all the chills and fevers of faith, along with everyone else.

The questions themselves are real enough, though often met by indifference instead of conclusion. The pages of this book reflect abiding convictions about the answer: The very marks of a secular day which make ministry difficult also make it imperative. Here in the secular setting, to a marked degree, are the very needs which pastoral practice addresses: to respect persons in the midst of impersonal systems; to know people by name who are becoming only numbers; to help men and women find joy beyond pleasure alone; to give a sense of belonging to people long since uprooted or never rooted; to provide horizons for life, behind us, before us, and above us.

The title is carefully chosen: "the authentic pastor." The word "authentic" according to the dictionary has three meanings, all close to our concern: (a) authoritative, (b) having a genuine origin, (c) trustworthy. In some dictionaries the explanatory note adds: "exactly that which the thing is said to be . . . thereby implying full trustworthiness." In all these ways we cherish the concept of the "authentic" pastor.

It is this authenticity which characterizes those who have left enduring marks upon our concept of the ministry. One of the most remarkable witnesses in this regard was the impact of Frederick W. Robertson of Brighton whose ministry in that English city was limited to six years because of his death. When, forty years later, his sermons were put into published form, his son wrote the introduction. Trying to put his hand on the secret of his father's influence, he said there were three things which remained in his memory about his father: "First, he was what he preached—true. Second, he was entirely in earnest. Third, he was essentially courageous."[1] What finer tribute could one receive from one's own son!

To clarify the meaning of that kind of authenticity in our secularized setting is the basic purpose of this book. Thus, this is not primarily a book on methods of pastoral work. It deals rather with the meanings of relationships and seeks to clarify some of the dynamics at work when any pastor ministers to persons. With a renewed sense of meaning in the ministry, a number of methods will prove useful. Without that meaning, none will, for any length of time.

It is my hope that in some sense this will prove a companion to an earlier volume, *The Audacity of Preaching*. I believe we are called to both, audacity in preaching and authenticity in pastoral care. To the extent that these pages give clarification to that call and provide support to those engaged in contemporary ministry, they will have carried out their intent.

GENE E. BARTLETT

Contents

Chapter 1

The Pastor's Search for Identity

As I turned away from the nurses' station and started down the corridor to the hospital room, it seemed one of the longest journeys I'd ever have to take. At the end of it was the need to help a man face death.

Two days before, at the request of a member of our congregation, I had called on a dentist who was facing surgery. We had not met before. Our first conversation had been casual enough, mostly the small talk of making contact.

In the intervening day the surgery had taken place. At the nurses' station the surgeon was writing in the record. When I identified myself as pastor to his patient, he shared the word with me. The surgery had revealed that the illness had advanced beyond recovery. Already the doctors had told him there was nothing more they could do.

With this word heavy on my mind I made my way to the room, wondering what anyone could say or do. Though ordained to the Christian ministry two years before, I found that ordination had not endowed me with the certainty, even the understanding, I needed so much in that moment.

Still wondering what to do, I pushed open the door to the room.

When the patient saw me, he picked up the subject immediately, "I suppose you have talked with the doctor?"

My answer was purposely ambiguous, "I saw him a few moments ago at the nurses' station."

There was a moment's pause as I waited to see where he wanted to go from there. "Well, it seems my number is up!" he said.

"The doctors told you that." It was a statement, not a question. "It only took one look," he said as his fingers traced a crease in the bed covers. "One look!" He traced the line in the cover for a moment more, then went on, "Well, it's all right. Oh, I'd like to see my twelve-year-old son grow up. And I'd like to know how some things turn out. But it's all right."

With no little wonder I realized in that moment that he already was finding his way through the first shock which had come to him. I marveled, as I was to marvel again and again in the years that followed, at the courage with which people go through such dark times in their lives.

For me, the questions raised that day about the meaning of the ministry were very real and in many ways disturbing. Shouldn't ministers know who they are and what they are to do? We can learn some things to *do,* learn them by sheer imitation, if necessary. But who will tell us *why* we do them? Who is a minister in the contemporary world anyway?

THE PREFAB ANSWERS

The culture itself will offer some ready-made answers if we're ready to take them without asking too many questions. Because life is generally easier if we can figure where each of us belongs, the culture has some niches prepared for every young minister.

People will make room for us, for example, if we are willing to become *keepers of the public morals.* We will keep an eye out for those things that threaten other people's traditional morals, especially those of our young people. It will be assumed that we are guardians of the traditions, custodians of those standards of behaviors which most people consider moral. Some of us can recall hilarious moments when in casual conversation it first was learned that we were ministers! The scramble to clean up language, to give the conversation a different tone, reflects what many think of a minister, a disclosure both tragic and comic at the same time.

Or, we can find a place as *chaplains to the culture.* Recent years have made us more aware of "civil religion"—a strange mixture of nostalgia and patriotism, of moral and spiritual values generally supporting the status quo, and of a certain kind of general religiosity using the religious terms as code words. Civil religion probably is the greatest single competitor to a genuine Christian faith in America. And it can be formidable competition. As Mark Twain once observed, "A ,well-put-together unreality is pretty hard to beat."

Civil religion will give us an identity of a kind. There always are invocations to give and committees on which we can represent religious interests. It even gives one the illusion of being a community leader, and that builds the ego.

Uncertainty about identity does not mean that we can't keep busy. We can. Sometimes the less certain we are about what we are to do, the more we do, perhaps hoping that somewhere in all that compulsive activity we may even hit on something real.

Or, third, *we can become organization persons.* Most of us belong to denominations which will keep us busy with packaged programs coming regularly to the pastor's desk. These are meant to be supplemental and suggestive; but they can be made substitutes for pastoral faithfulness which is responsive and personal.

There also will be occasions when you will be asked to *intercede as a spiritual ombudsman,* "saying a little prayer" or supposedly using your inside influence with the Divine. In this, one usually belongs to the emergency squad.

We can fill our days with these things. But we can't fill our hearts. For most of us, the failure to find real and deeper meaning of ministry leaves us feeling increasingly trivial and at least demeaned. Or we feel we are playing a role, theatrically speaking, and are really an illusion created by devices and stratagems. It is a painful, even critical time, when that moment of self-disclosure comes.

In his book, *Seven Storey Mountain,* Thomas Merton tells of his spiritual pilgrimage, a seeking which led him, by the time the book was written, to become a Trappist monk. Along the way, hoping for some guidance, he sought out a Protestant minister. But he came away empty and disappointed. Of that minister Merton wrote, "You felt that the man did not know his vocation, did not know what he was supposed to be. He had taken upon himself some function in society which was not his and which was, indeed, not a necessary function at all.[1]

After these years in the ministry, I'm persuaded that the need to understand who we are and what we do and why we do it is a lifelong unfinished business. To abandon the inquiry, to close off one's life, and to settle for repetitious imitations in ministry is to miss one of life's most exciting—and demanding—experiences. Though it certainly doesn't need to, the ministry can grow trivial and trite. One wonders how many pastors feel that way about themselves and vaguely hope there's some chance to get back to something meaningful.

It is reported that one day Emerson and Thoreau were talking about their alma mater, Harvard. "Well," said Emerson, "I see Harvard now teaches all the branches of knowledge." Thoreau came back with a typical Thoreau reply, "Yes, all the branches and none of the roots!" To sense that this has happened in ministry is to make the search for real identity urgent indeed, yes, even critical.

A CONTEMPORARY IDENTITY

Then, where is identity to be found? This is such a basic question that it will evoke a variety of historic answers, each probably reflecting some tradition within the church. We certainly are not without measured thought on the subject, nor without any witnesses. Yet, having heard what others have said, we in this secular time must find the answer for ourselves. For the question has never been asked *from the place where we ourselves stand.* While that probably has been true at every point in history, it seems more radically true now when the secular has become sovereign, not only in theory but also in fact. Secularism is in the very unexamined assumptions by which people live. Most of us in fact are secular even when we never use its words. We simply grew up in a secular climate.

Again, then, where is identity to be found? The very term "identity" implies that one is *identified with* something. But with what? Though I cannot pinpoint a time, there emerged in my ministry an answer which has deepened and grown over the years. It seems to me biblically and theologically grounded and at the same time practically applicable to our everyday human experiences. Though it is far from precise, often opening more questions than it answers—but different and deeper questions—this concept has proved consistently helpful, giving me some understanding when I needed it most. In part, it is an answer to the question foremost in my mind when I walked down that hospital corridor all those years ago.

This concept is expressed in one of the most familiar phrases in the

New Testament: "the ministry of reconciliation." I did not discover the meaning of pastoral practice from reading the words; I discovered the meaning of the words from engagement in pastoral practice. One day practice and words came together, and the term "ministry of reconciliation" has illumined my daily work ever since.

"Reconciliation" in the Greek has a commercial origin. It seems to have referred to the exchange of coins of equal value. It meant, in short, a fair exchange. After the manner of language it began to take on deeper meanings. Today it stands not only for itself but also for a whole family of words, some of the best in human experience: harmony, oneness, making peace, coming to terms with, and overcoming alienation. Seen in this light it broadens out into a word with many affiliations. It moves like a healing stream through all of life, touching every experience.

RECONCILIATION TOUCHES ALL LIFE

This wider meaning is essential to understanding our thesis. It may further that understanding to speak of some points in life where reconciliation is commonly needed: to one another, to one's self, to changed conditions of life, to work, and to God. Pastors will find themselves involved in all these human conditions.

There is a need for *reconciliation between persons.* Alienation is a harsh word, and an even harsher experience. To be estranged, especially after being close, means pain and sometimes terror. The cries of alienation sound all through our culture, in the literature, in the biographies, and in the formal studies made by social scientists. But we're not thinking here about alienation as a social phenomenon. We think of it as something that happens to those about whom we care, something which left unattended can prove so destructive as to ruin lives. While often chronic, alienation can become an emergency or a crisis. Because of it people come apart not only from one another but also within themselves. To find reconciliation is one form of what it means to be "saved," for it is just that.

I recall with great sadness families who never found reconciliation and as a result destroyed not only the family unit but also the persons themselves, even into the second generation. A dispute over distribution of an inheritance once brought tension to a family; then the tension brought a breaking point. Over the years almost every person suffered mental and physical damage from that malignant alienation! At first, they were not reconciled because they wouldn't;

then the time came when they were not reconciled because they couldn't. Talk about judgment! But talk about grace, too, blessed grace which by reconciliation can put a halt to the terrible damage of estrangement.

Not all reconciliation is as urgent as that. There are lesser reconciliations which bring harmony instead of disharmony to life. A music teacher gave me an interesting illustration of that. She said that each musical note has its own vibration. But when two notes are sounded in harmony, it is not a case of two vibrations sounding at once. It is a whole new vibration! Each has given up its own for something new. The pastor will often share that process between persons, the finding of new interdependence by which life matures.

But we need to see also that this maturity requires *reconciliation to oneself*. Self-acceptance is a fairly easy word to use, but it is far from easy to fulfill.

It is revealing to know that an earlier day often called a psychiatrist an "alienist." That carries an insight of its own, for often disturbed persons have become alien to themselves. Most of us experience some degree of conflict between what we are and what we want to be, between what others see in us and what we feel ourselves to be, sometimes between what we wish we were and what we find we really are. One way or another we have to come to terms with ourselves, often "to make peace with ourselves." At that point the pastor who will enter into that process lovingly and patiently can help another in that process of coming to terms with oneself. Such times are way stations to maturity.

There also seems to be a need to be *reconciled to one's daily work*. This caught me by surprise early in my ministry when through a weekly radio program I invited people to write or come in and talk about their problems. Next to the family, the daily work was the area of more conflicts than any other. Often it was the seemingly degrading nature of the work itself or of the relationship to someone in the work situation.

This has been confirmed by a recent book by Studs Terkel entitled *Working*. In the introduction, Terkel, recalling hundreds of interviews on all phases of life, says, "[This] is above all (or beneath all), about daily humiliations. To survive the day is triumph enough for the walking wounded among the great many of us."[2] To come to terms, one way or another, with the working relation (or with retirement) is reconciliation to a major part of one's life.

Beyond that are the needs to be reconciled to *conditions of life which cannot be changed.* The life cycle moves on inexorably and with it come not only the fulfillments but the frustrations. This truth comes to one of its clearest manifestations in the middle years of life. Many pastors are finding that a growing portion of counseling and care is needed by those in the very decade of life where they expected to "have it made." But often when the forties come, personal experiences converge to make it a time of special stress.

If the marriage has had strains, they tend to come to the most intense form in these middle years, and real reconciliation between husband and wife may be needed. It is a time when teenage breaking away may also become intense, leaving both parents and children hurt and baffled. These same years may require added care for one's aging parents. One must also be reconciled to other conditions of middlessence: plateaus in work or profession, perhaps the threat of financial insecurity, reminders that powers one has counted on soon will begin to wane. Over all there is a general feeling that time is running out.

It's a familiar picture, poignant and touching. In almost all aspects of the middle years the need is reconciliation: with those one loves most, with the fact of change, the evidence of time's inexorable moving.

Bereavement, invalidism, separation, and aging are close to any pastor's practice. People react to all of these in a number of ways— from denial, to attack, to panic, to depression. To be reconciled to that unchangeable condition, whether it is a condition of ill health or broken relationships, does not mean surrendering to it. It means absorbing it into one's life. When such problems come, the question is whether the person will absorb the problem or the problem will absorb the person. The former is victory, the latter defeat.

It is said that a friend of Ruskin once spilled something on a favorite scarf leaving a stain which could not be removed. Seeing her distress, Ruskin asked to borrow the scarf for a few days. When he returned it, the blot had not been removed but had been included in a new design. Working with the unwanted spot, he had made it part of the design with symmetry and beauty. That this can happen in the unchangeable conditions we all face is part of the promise of our Christian faith.

Including all these, but more, is our *reconciliation with God.* While few would disagree with such words, many feel they do not understand them. God language is a foreign language for many in a secular day. But the basic experience is there even when we don't use the words. T. S. Eliot caught the mood well when he caused Celia to say in *The Cocktail Party,*

> It's not the feeling of anything I've ever *done,*
> Which I might get away from or anything in me
> I could get rid of—but of emptiness, of failure
> Towards someone, or something, outside of myself;
> And I feel I must . . . *atone*—is that the word?
> Can you treat a patient for such a state of mind?[3]

It is not surprising that many do not use the words of piety to express their need for reconciliation with God. We are more likely to speak of "something missing," "something wrong." We wonder at our emptiness in the midst of so much, or at our loneliness when surrounded by so many. We are surprised by our satiation when we expected satisfaction, or at our uncertainty about our worth when we possess so much. And nothing we can do takes away the reminder that mortality looks over our shoulder even in the most successful enterprise. Where then are the fruits of the Spirit—love, joy, and peace?

To help another person deal with this feeling without imposing words that have no meaning or surface solutions that have no reality is to enter into a demanding, searching, and very human relationship. To share another's seeking for God has pain in it and many times a feeling of powerlessness. This reality brings into the open the shallowness of some forms of evangelism. They are promotional, not pastoral. They settle for new labels not new birth. Real evangelism is much nearer courtship than salesmanship. It respects times and seasons and knows when to wait upon God.

Helping another come to know God or to find meaning in life is pastoral in the fullest sense of the word. While God obviously can reconcile any person to himself in his own way and time, the probability is that he does it through other persons. To be ready to be that person, to love and care and reach out, demanding no timetable and no stock answer, is the ministry of reconciliation at its deepest level. The great words of faith will follow in due time when one has had an experience which needs a name.

THE SUSTAINING FAITH

This brings us to the heart of the matter, namely, the faith by which such a ministry is sustained. For the only ground on which a pastoral relationship can be authentic is the theological one. It is the belief—and it's an audacious one—"that God was in Christ reconciling" and is now continuing that ministry. Without that assumption any ministry on our part becomes rootless and limited.

It is possible, of course, to have a pastoral ministry of a kind without the theological assumption. It then becomes another form of human relationship, hopefully helpful as one person can help another, but deprived of the main hope which rests in God's work, not ours. Is that hope of God's help foolish? Is it fantasy, not reality?

It is helpful to recall that most human endeavor is a partnership with powers beyond ourselves. The physician removes obstacles to healing and gives every support to the processes, but only powers not created by the doctor bring the healing. The parent tries to learn the skills of parenting, entering into that process to take on both its joys and triumphs. But growth itself is something given, a power that cannot be commanded but only guided. The farmer plants a field, using all the knowledge and accumulated experience at hand, but fertility of the earth is given, the assumption upon which the work is done.

It is not inconsistent with our total experience, therefore, for the pastor to take up a ministry of reconciling, believing God already is at work, the Author and Finisher of that redemption.

In this regard pastors can speak of "that which we have seen and heard." We constantly encounter a power at work beyond ourselves. We go to a home where bereavement has come, often wondering what can be said or done. But there we find One has gone before us. Comfort and strength have been given—and we didn't give it. We witnessed it, and we amplified it; but we did not give it. Or in counseling we enter into the pain, the searching, the burden of another and even share that one's helplessness. But in that counseling, if we learn to look for the signs, there come *emergences,* new things that could not have been expected—insights, releases, confidences. And you know these are the *gifts,* usually not a "sudden rending of the veil of clay" but moments that took "the dimness of my soul away." The belief that God is at work reconciling is not a matter to be believed because it is written in a book. That belief best describes what the pastor sees who lives out the calling in everyday practice.

Pastoral practice then rests on the same foundation as the practice of the Christian life itself. Apart from the belief in an active, loving, redemptive God, intimately at work in human experience, the whole Christian life loses its distinction and becomes a human experience only, of high order, to be sure, but only human. But the Christian life is not a way of calling out something in ourselves only, but of calling upon Him who is beyond ourselves. The new life is new because it has become a partnership, life reoriented in the light of a relationship.

So it is with pastoral practice. The pastor becomes mediator and witness to something beyond the human relationship alone. That is one meaning, I believe, of the priesthood of all believers.

The belief in that redemptive power at work on our behalf is described in William James's classic work on *The Varieties of Religious Experience.* Speaking of one who has come to such a saving experience James says, *"He becomes conscious that this higher part is conterminous and continuous with a* MORE *of the same quality, which is operative in the universe outside of him, and which he can keep in working touch with, and in a fashion get on board of and save himself. . . ."*[4] The language is not the kind we use, but it describes the reality which gives pastoral care its deepest dimension, beyond the warm and caring personal relationship, important as that is. The pastor's work is understood as the attempt to help needy people get in touch with that "more" we call the power of God.

This means that, like the practice of the Christian life itself, pastoral practice is really an act of faith, a faith which will seek every insight, learn every skill human research can provide but at last trusts the "more" of which James speaks. The faith that God is at work in human life is not a release from our responsibility, but the reason for our working in hope, not suspending the clinical skills which have become valued tools of pastoral practice, but certainly transcending them.

THE HIDDEN HUNGER

Every week for several years I called on a member of our congregation who was in a nursing home. To reach her room, I passed the open door of another room and often noticed a woman in a wheelchair seated by the window. When I stopped one day to greet her, I saw that paralysis had robbed her of her ability to speak. Yet each time I stopped at her door, spoke to her, then went on to make my call.

One day after I had greeted her in this way, something caught my attention on my way out. When I stopped at the door for the second time, by inarticulate sound and movements of her head it was evident that she wanted me to come in. When I stood beside her chair, she nodded to the pencil tablet on her lap. I picked it up to discover that she had managed to scrawl a single word in large letters: "Prayer." It brought back poignant memories of all the times I had stopped by her doorway and engaged in some passing small talk! All the time she had waited and hoped for the "more" which prayer assumes.

Though the years have been many since this episode took place, the understanding has endured. The years since have brought constant reminders and witness to the hope that God is in the world reconciling, and that he is the "more" in every human condition. To know that he has given us the ministry of reconciliation is to take a major step toward understanding who we are and what we are to do. In this faith are both our identity and our credentials.

Chapter 2

Ministering in the Secular Climate

In his classic biography of Phillips Brooks, Alexander V. G. Allen studies with special interest the second year of Brooks's divinity school experience. Brooks had entered theological school defeated and uncertain, having failed in his first intent to be a teacher. Tentatively, he had gone to theological school, but the whole first year had been marked by the sense of defeat and uncertainty he had brought with him.

In that second year, however, new things appeared in his life. Out of the defeated teacher came the emerging preacher. In the biographer's view, that second year was the changing point in the life of Brooks. Summing it up, Allen says, "It is a conversion so deep, so thorough, as to find its precedents only in the conversion of an Augustine or a Luther . . . , while yet it differs from them as the nineteenth century differs from the fourth century or the sixteenth." [1]

It is a provocative insight. It reminds us that Christian experience in any generation is a combination of the timeless and the timely. In that sense, each generation's experience is unique, for that particular combination of time and the timeless never has taken place before. In our time the particular combination seems to be the intersection of the priority of secular concerns and the gospel.

THE SECULAR INTERSECTION

Whether we use these words or not, most of us have the feeling of standing at an intersection, and a busy one at that. One way or another our intersection is where we encounter secularism. Surely the prevailing view of life in our time is this-worldly, thing-centered, and given to the pursuit of self-sufficiency.

Formal theology long has been engaged in the debate about secularity even before it filtered down into our common life. Theology has had to come to terms with secularism, which Gabriel Fackre describes in summarizing William Hamilton's position, as "stress on the possibilities rather than the impossibilities of this world and this time, and a movement of the center of gravity of theological thought and Christian life from the academy and temple to the street."[2]

As pastors we meet secularism at another level—in the daily assumptions by which people live, in the way in which we divide our time, in the values we assume, and in the ends we pursue. Most of all we see it in what we trust. This is the intersection of pastoral experience.

Early in my ministry I was confronted one night by an articulate secularist. We were having a class in preparation of adults for church membership. A couple who happened to be strolling through the neighborhood saw the lights in the church and came in, expecting a public meeting. We explained the nature of our group and invited them to stay. To our surprise, they accepted. They sat through the discussion in which I was trying to interpret the Christian faith. When the meeting was opened for questions, our visitor asked if he could say a word. It was both a question and a statement: "I have listened with real interest to what you have said because I *want* to know what the Christian faith is. But you haven't put it in a language I can understand. You use some sort of philosophical terms. At least I suppose they are philosophical. But, you see, that's not a language I understand. Not at all! I'm an engineer. I've been overseas searching for some new oil fields. As an engineer I'm trained to measure things. I understand them only when I can measure or test them. That's the only way I can think. Who can help ME understand what the Christian faith is?"

In my imagination that man has sat in every congregation to which I have preached since! How do you make clear the Christian faith to someone schooled in the secular ways of looking at things?

This is not to say that secularism is something *wrong*. It isn't. To the contrary, its benefits to human life have been immense, beyond our measuring. Through science, which is the mainstream of the secular view, our lives have been prolonged and protected, and our communication can carry a whisper around the world. We have been given wings to go in hours to even the remotest parts of the world. Given the choice, almost all of us would take our secular time over any other. It has made us giants in the earth.

Then why don't we settle for it? What's all the fuss? Haven't we entered a new age where the secular at last is sufficient? For the pastor that question has to be faced not in terms of ideas alone, but in terms of persons. What happens to us?

What happens to us is that we get lost and let down. We become idolaters, for our goods become our gods. In chapter 44 of Isaiah the prophet draws a timeless picture of a worshiper of idols. He describes a man who grows a good tree in the forest, then cuts it down and brings it out for his use. Because he is cold, he takes the first part to make a fire to warm himself. Then finding he is hungry, he uses most of the remainder to cook his dinner. Thus when he is warm and fed, says Isaiah, "he is satisfied." Then he discovers that he has a few scraps of wood left. One of these he carves into an idol and falls down to worship it. "You are my god, deliver me." Because the idol was carved from scraps, Isaiah says in fine satire, "The residue thereof he maketh a god" (Isaiah 44:17, KJV).

It is striking to note how Jesus reversed that order of things. In the Sermon on the Mount he taught those who would follow him not to be anxious about what they would eat, or drink, or wear, for "your heavenly Father knoweth that ye have need of all these things." Then he set the priority. "Seek ye first the kingdom of God, and his righteousness; and all these things shall be added unto you" (Matthew 6:32, 33, KJV). The conflict between secularism and the Christian faith is in these contrasting orders: God in first place, sovereign; or in last, residue.

FOUR BASIC HUMAN NEEDS

Pastorally speaking, the secular approach to life becomes "secularism" when it seeks to fulfill the basic spiritual needs in persons. These needs appear in an amazing number of variations. But they are urgent and constant. Those needs are: to find the good life, to belong, to relate to a trustworthy authority, and to overcome alienation. Each deserves our consideration.

First, there is *the need to find the good life.* The secular view promises, even promotes, the good life—on its own terms. An airline recently made this promise its advertising slogan. I first became aware of it when making a trip from Boston to Chicago. After I had checked in, I noticed that over the door leading to the plane were the words "To the good life." And I thought I was just going to Chicago! I doubt if even the Chicago Chamber of Commerce would make such a bold claim. My ticket wasn't even first class! The good life on a coach ticket?

The slogan didn't appear out of nowhere. It's the theme pressed upon us again and again by advertising. How many products are offered not for what they can do, but for what they can do for us! The secular view, promoted at great cost in sophisticated advertising, is that the good life comes by getting spiritual results from material things.

Listen to advertising. A new car is "something to believe in." One page had the heading "Key to a better life." Dangling in the middle of the page was the key to a new car! Some of it sounds precisely like evangelism: "Datsun saves. It sets you free." Things are sold not so much by the promise of utility or durability or efficiency, but by the promise that they will give us confidence, distinction, a feeling of success, and often sexual attraction. The good life of secularism is not by grace but by getting.

Jesus reserved one of his hardest words for a man who tried to get spiritual results from material things. He told of the farmer who had a bumper crop one year, so abundant that he had to build extra barns to contain it. When his barns were full to overflowing, he went out to look at them. Surveying his plenty, he didn't affirm that now he would have enough to share with his neighbor, or even that he had more than enough for his physical needs. Seeing the overflowing barns, he said, "Soul . . . take your ease." Jesus' word is blunt. "Fool! This night your soul is required of you!" (Luke 12:19, 20).

In our own way, we are finding a kind of judgment which comes from supposing that the good life can be realized in secular and material terms alone. We find ourselves living under a law of our own, as real as that of Paul, but vastly different. For the secular law is that of self-sufficiency. In the secular view the law is that we must be self-sufficient and the gospel is that we can be. Under that cruel law and false gospel lives are being lost every day.

Many begin another day's work supposing that if they just get one more promotion, they will "have it made." Or if they win one more recognition, they will find the inner assurance they seek. Or if they gain a little more power, then they will know inner security at last. It is a tragic and destructive falsehood, taking its toll in human happiness and welfare. At this point the secular person comes close to pastoral concern. Those living under the secular law of self-sufficiency are already under judgment and stand in urgent need of God's grace!

The second evident spiritual condition seen in a secular culture is *the need to belong.* The same communications revolution which opens the world to us leaves us not sure where we belong in it. Perhaps the intensity of the peer loyalties of youth and the ethnic togetherness of minorities comes in part from that need to belong.

Alfred Toffler in his *Future Shock* points out that our very mobility contributes to rootlessness. Every year about forty million Americans make a move. Toffler reminds us that this exceeds in volume any of the great migrations of history and yet it takes place every year.[3] Such incessant coming and going makes clear what one character in a contemporary play meant when he said, "I am a permanent transient."

Practically, this has a marked effect upon our church life. In some churches there is a word of invitation at the close of a service. We proclaim that "the doors of this church are open." We mean, of course, open for those who wish to come in. But increasingly it seems also open for those who need to go out! The doors of the church are indeed open, entrance and exit. Most churches need to take in a number equal to 10 percent of their membership each year just to hold their own.

It sometimes is difficult for pastors to accept the fact that many people prefer *not* to belong to anything. The freedom not to relate is also a human freedom made possible in a secular day. There are those for whom not belonging is far easier emotionally. They have all the relationships they can handle, even though to others their lives seem limited. In a city church where we invited registration, each Sunday we received a rather constant number of visitors' cards. But when we made a survey in which one did not have to sign a name, we found there were twice as many visitors as we had supposed. Anonymity is one of the new possibilities in a mobile urban society, and many take refuge in it.

This inner conflict between belonging and not belonging may well be one of the most common conflicts of secular man. What is clear is that *choice* has been given. If once we commonly found our place in communities of our birth, increasingly we find communities by the right of choice.

It is profoundly important to see that belonging in the church is a distinctive form of belonging. It is not a social group which only provides a chance to be with people. The church has not taken form because "the more we get together, the happier we will be." The church is a distinctive community of faith, having both a memory and a mission. It simply transcends the usual separations of time or culture or place. It lives out the faith that Christ is living. Where we gather in his name, he speaks his word and carries out his work. To be sure, there is a superficial membership in the church. The real belonging comes only when one is "in Christ," in a community of faith carrying the memory and mission of Jesus Christ.

Where there is that hunger to belong, as many in a secular culture come to feel, then the church with this particular faith can be a discovery, a "coming home" in the fullest sense of that word.

Third, for many there is *the need to relate to a trustworthy authority.* Each aspect of life tends to develop its own autonomy. Giving to science, art, and education the right to govern themselves and to develop their own standards was a mark of the modern era. This freedom brought a tremendous leap forward in most fields of knowlege and experience. People in these fields found it to be an especially liberating experience to get out from under the control of the church. Many feel it is yet to be shown whether these disciplines, fleeing from an authoritarian church, did not run full into the arms of secular authorities—the state or the corporation.

This means that in their everyday experience people can feel segmented, even fragmented. A young man driving me to the airport after a speaking engagement told me he had dropped out of college. He had been doing well, and he had adequate financial support. Yet he had taken some time off to "find himself." When asked why, he said, "There are so many options and no one has told me how to know which is better than another." Toffler calls it "overchoice."

Especially difficult for many is the fact that this pluralism now has emerged in moralities and life-styles. I'm persuaded that this freedom of choice is better, making for maturity. But it also is confusing and often full of conflict. How can anyone know which is best? What is the criterion? Perhaps one reason the adolescent stage of life—no long-term commitments in work or marriage—has lengthened out is that the options are so many. One doesn't want to close them off too soon.

Often we do not see that the secular view of life has required us all to make more choices, sometimes very basic choices about our values and our life-styles. From our perspective it seems that other times had more grooves and niches into which all were expected to fit. In our pluralism we are not compelled to conform, but we are compelled to choose.

Yet this is a condition in which the biblical faith should feel at home, for the note of decision is sounded again and again in the biblical story. When there are so many gospels and so many authorities, the biblical word comes to us with newness and freshness: "Choose you this day whom you will serve." Pastoral preaching and counseling can help make clear the necessity of that choice, the possibility of it, and, hopefully, support those who are making it.

For some there seem to be more choices than they can handle. A secular culture which has increased the options, including ways of life, and become increasingly uncertain about criteria is bound to produce Toffler's "overchoice." But it's not clear whether that feeling is really "overchoice" or "under criteria." The result is a widespread, almost epidemic indifference which finally settles upon us, especially upon our young people, usually around high school age. The sociologist speaks of "anomie" as one of the discernible marks of our time. It implies a lack of standards, a loss of verve and nerve, a vague, undefined malaise. Is this, in part, from too many options and too few criteria?

It is at this point that Christ confronts a secular culture where people are in need. There is no way to experience the Christian life apart from choice and that demand goes on all through life. Holman Hunt's famous picture shows Jesus knocking at the door waiting for response. But once inside, there are other doors, other rooms, and he goes from one to the other. Our temptation is to let Christ step inside the front door, but to keep him there. In fact, he knocks at every door: vocation, family, recreation, old traumas, new fears. But only we can let him in. The basic commitment is a choice in the midst of many competitive gospels and alternative ways.

The fourth human need which emerges in a secular culture is *the need to overcome alienation.* Whether our personal isolation is more real than in other generations is not clear. Men and women never were required to relate to as many kinds of people as in this day when by communication and transportation we have become a global, or at least, a national village. There are so many more to relate to! And some are so different!

So for countless numbers of people life is experienced as separation or apartness, as alienation or isolation. It is now well documented and often said that we easily become nameless, having numbers instead of names. But it is deeper than that. Even when we have names, there is the hunger for knowing and being known, the hunger for intimacy. Though such closeness is not possible with many, life is impoverished when some closeness is not present, even with a few.

Thomas Wolfe on his thirtieth birthday fell into a contemplative mood. In a document of reflection on his birthday he includes the query, "In the course of my . . . thirty years of living, how many people had I seen? How many had I passed by on the streets? . . . With how many had I actually had some vital and illuminating experience, whether of joy, pain, anger, pity, love, or simple casual companionship, however brief?"[4]

It is significant that in response to this need there has been a discernible rise in the number of small groups, some in the church, some outside. Sometimes these groups center upon a particular common experience, such as divorce and separation. Sometimes they are support groups for those passing through a transition time. Sometimes they are groups concerned for mutual growth. Pastoral concern welcomes these as significant resources for mutual help. These groups mark one of the growing dimensions of pastoral care, a response to the secular mood in which we live. Such small groups help to reduce the alienation from one another which we experience and to build stronger human relationships.

The depth of our sense of separation is seen in the truth that for many separation is descriptive of their experience of God. If our personal experience were not enough witness in itself, our literature and drama certainly would reveal it. There seems little doubt that in our time God is experienced in terms of his absence, his distance, and even his "death." Strangely enough, the experience of God's absence is one form of "knowing God." We don't sense the absence of that which has not been present. If we know he's gone, we must know that he has been here! Many of us have to confess that our most real experience of God at this point is the feeling of separation, the sense of his absence.

LOOK WHO'S COMING!

To speak of these needs is not to imply that the secular is our enemy. To the contrary, like the New Testament Christians we can look forward "with eager longing for the revealing of the sons of God" (Romans 8:19) in a secular order. For we can believe that God IS bringing forth something new, a new manifestation of the Christian life, shaped in part by the very secular day in which we receive the gospel anew. We can affirm that surely God's purpose for persons now is not to take us back to what we have been, but to lead us on to what we have not yet been.

After all, when we hear the promise that "if anyone is in Christ, he is a new creation" (2 Corinthians 5:17), we may suppose that doesn't mean another *copy*. It means a new *creation,* an original! We who work and preach at the intersection of the gospel with the secular should look with real eagerness to what the evangelized secular person will be!

The Christian manifesto in our secular time was spoken to the Corinthians all those years ago: "All things are yours . . . and you are Christ's" (1 Corinthians 3:21-23). All things—the powers, the knowledge, the freedoms, the personal status, the sheer enjoyments which mark the time. All are yours! But, you are Christ's. That's the redemptive word, the saving center. To find that balance is one purpose of pastoral care in our time. It's our ministry to secular men and women.

That word gives great promise of a fresh manifestation of the good news with dimensions we've never had before, dimensions which are themselves our faith's response to the secular challenge.

Chapter 3

Distinctive Resources for Pastoral Practice

Sometimes it must seem that the question mark is the sign of the times for the contemporary pastor. It confronts us on every side. Already we have noted that we have to ask with new urgency: Who am I? We further have considered the demanding query: What kind of culture is the contemporary setting for our ministry? Now we have to face an equally pressing question: What are the distinctive resources with which the pastor works?

In a time so clearly marked by specialization, pastors often feel vague and ill-defined. While others have developed the science of measurement to an infinitesimal degree, we still deal with the immeasurable. When most professions have developed precision of procedure, the pastor still seems locked into imprecision. So, with what *does* one work?

As we become aware of this troublesome feeling, we tend to do one of several things: We may try to imitate those who have more defined resources and precise procedures. We may determine that we will act professionally even when we don't feel like it! Or we gradually develop a feeling of inferiority. We conclude that if our resources can't be defined more clearly, they must not be very effective.

But neither of these options really works in the long run. That's when we find there is an alternative with promise, even excitement. It is to let other callings have their resources and make full use of them. Some of them are impressive indeed and have been finely fashioned to bless persons with new health of body and emancipation of mind. But it is important for pastors to take a renewed look at their calling and see again how distinctive and impressive are the resources available to the minister as minister. These resources are so genuinely needed that it is sheer tragedy to overlook them and to spend wasted energy on envy of others. The pastor is *not* without tools! To the contrary, we have instruments of helping especially relevant to a secular day.

It is said that a passing remark gave impetus to Evangeline Booth in her establishment of the Salvation Army. She was being shown through a factory which made glass. The guide took her to a room full of unusually fine glass pieces. "No tool can do these," said the guide. "These require the human touch." Evangeline Booth knew in that moment that helping other people also requires "the human touch." It sent her back to the work of the Salvation Army with new insight. The resources of the pastor are that "human touch."

It is said that older maps of the Pacific designed for navigation by sea had some areas with an interesting marking. Around clusters of dots the legend said, "Islands owned but not occupied." We would be losers indeed if the resources available to pastoral practice were thus described: "Owned but not occupied."

Then what does the pastor have at hand? Human needs are so poignant that they face us with a question God asked of Moses, when Moses, wanting to set his people free, still faltered in inadequacy. God said to him, "What is that in your hand?" That's where we have to start, too.

FIVE DISTINCTIVE RESOURCES OF THE PASTOR

There are some answers, and they intrigue us. Resources available to the pastor cannot be found anywhere else, at least in similar combination, in my judgment. Any one of the resources is greatly to be valued. Together they give a synergistic energy impressive and redemptive in the human situation. I believe there are five relationships which go with the pastoral calling. In these we find the means of our ministry.

1. The Presumption of Trust

Trust seems to be a diminishing reality in our contemporary scene.

Is that in part the result of advertising which corrupts words, using them with studied sophistication to practice deception? Increasingly one senses the mounting suspicion which runs through our commercial life. Our very systems seem to be fashioned by suspicion instead of trust. Underlying so many new procedures is the presumption of an intention to defraud. In most of our common life then trust is becoming a rare commodity.

Perhaps that's one reason a real trust relationship is so fulfilling when it *is* found. We all feel more human because of it.

The point here is that the pastor by the nature of the calling *begins* with the presumption of trustworthiness. Moreover, that presumption is offered to a pastor by a group of people who join together in extending the invitation. Most others who relate to persons have to build that trust, person by person, encounter by encounter. The pastor, on the other hand, is called by a community of people who already have been convinced of his or her trustworthiness. The call itself, then, becomes an act of confidence.

It must be added immediately that such trust while presumed can be lost in short order. The pastor's manner of life, the integrity of word and ways, the evidences of faithfulness in the various forms of ministry—all these at last can be the confirmation of the presumption. Or the lack of these things can destroy trust, so that the presumption is withdrawn. Failure to pick up the option is a tragic loss to both the minister and the congregation. In a world which offers little enough trust the loss of pastoral trust becomes a deep disappointment.

This means that some personal practices become important not only for themselves but also for validating the trustworthiness which has been assumed. One of those practices, of course, is the strictest respect for confidences given. Any evidence that the minister has revealed directly or indirectly any confidential word entrusted to him or her lowers the level of confidence immediately. Even with the presumption of trust, people need confirming evidence that the confidence is well placed. It must be realized that those who need a confidential relationship most are supersensitive by the very nature of the problems they carry. The same problem which produces the need also produces hypersensitivity and a poised readiness to scamper away if there is any doubt at all about confidentiality. To the needy even the whisper of disclosure becomes in their ears a shout. Fear is one of the symptoms of the problem, usually a fear of disclosure and the loss of face. It takes unusual evidence of confidentiality to keep the door open. The one needing pastoral care is usually wanting and fearing help at the same time. The need for reassurance about confidentiality is heightened by the fact that the pastor is also a preacher. There are aspects of the preaching ministry which are strongly supportive to pastoral care but at this point, where confidentiality is being tested, preaching has its own hazards. Sometimes preachers are tempted to use a "disguised" personal conversation or episode to illustrate a point. The minister may even be tempted to suppose that by making it known that someone else has come to talk with him or her, others may be encouraged to do so. In the main, I'm persuaded such practice has a reverse effect. At that point the person wanting help quietly decides not to risk it—not caring to be the illustration in *next* Sunday's sermon. Thus because the pastor is dealing with supersensitivity, one in return must practice super-caution.

Another way in which the trust relationship can be confirmed is in the lowly and often routine committee meetings. Lay people sometimes get their best insights into their ministers when they are out of the pulpit and sitting at the table helping to order the life of the church. Here ministers really disclose more than they know, their respect for the opinion of others, their reaction to opposition, their peevish petulance when things don't go right, the unconscious self-seeking or special pleading which has a way of cropping out when they least expect, the actual depth of their caring. Thus in the repeated contacts within the small group, ministers often show their hands—and their hearts.

Once more, it is important for the minister to come to terms with the neurotic tendencies which all of us have. These tendencies, unknown, unaccepted, or unclarified, can encumber and even destroy a ministry over the years. None of us can expect to avoid such inner conflicts that mark all human experience: the hostilities we accumulate, the excessive demand for adulation, the threatened security in the face of opposition, and the deep-rooted anxieties which many of us carry all of our lives. When those tendencies take over, we find ourselves demanding to be ministered unto. Our hungry ego needs or our painful traumas make their own demands upon us, and we tend to make them in turn on our congregations.

To come to terms with these emotional needs is essential to any mature ministry which confirms the trust of which we speak.

Theological education must include some opportunity for personal counseling, individually or in support groups, for the minister to get himself or herself together. No small part of the creative energy of the ministry can be derived from the process of transmuting these personal pains into compassion. A minister can come to love the people of his congregation in a way not unlike that which Elizabeth Barrett Browning confessed for Robert, "with all the passion put to use in my old griefs." Redeemed personal pain can give a quality to ministry difficult to define but essential to confirm the trust relationship.

At the last, then, trust offered at the outset to the minister is a gift, but it has to be cherished and confirmed. Then it becomes a resource of immeasurable worth.

2. The Ministry of Presence

None of us wants to be merely a symbol. Something deep inside every person insists that one should be accepted for oneself. But in the reality of human experience each of us "stands for something." Usually related to our calling, each of us represents an area of human life. The doctor represents the forces of healing; the teacher represents knowledge; the politician represents government in one of its several forms.

Consistent with this is the fact that the minister does represent the "spiritual resources" of life. The ministry of a pastor is far more than personal influence. It rests upon the belief that there is, noted earlier in the words of William James, the "More on which we can get on board." As the physician represents forces of healing that are outside himself or herself, so the pastor represents the transcendent powers to which we reach out in our times of need.

Some will rebel against the symbolic nature of the pastoral role. It is not easy to be a symbol! But it seems to me that the more mature minister will accept this fact and seek to keep it close to reality. If the pastor did not share the belief in those transcendent powers, it would be false and deceptive to accept the role. But when one does believe that there are such powers in life, and that a part of the ministry is helping other people find them, then the symbolic nature of the ministry becomes a part of the mediating role. In that sense it becomes one of the "givens" distinctive to the calling.

There is a strange arithmetic about the pastoral office. The arithmetic formula, $1 + 1 = 2$, becomes on occasion in the spiritual realm, 1 + 1 = 3. The pastor often will see the fulfillment of the promise "Where two or three are gathered in my name, there am I in the midst."

What we are speaking of here is the ministry of presence. It would not be possible if it were not for the representative nature of the pastoral office. How many times a pastor will be surprised by the help imparted simply by being there! It cannot be explained as the effect of one person upon another, though there are times when that in itself is important. It has to be understood, in my judgment, as the mediating effect of what one stands for as a pastor.

A part of the faith experience is reaching out to that which is beyond ourselves. It's the very essence of the religious experience. In recent days, Jimmy Breslin, in his book *How the Good Guys Finally Won*, brought in a surprising observation about the Watergate days. As a Catholic, Breslin wrote:

> These ceremonies of the religion—the Confession, the liturgical services—form a third-party intermediary; but with no way to externalize his evil, Nixon had only himself. Therefore, with no outward doctrine calling for the continual planning for failure, for sin, Nixon was unprepared for failure. Always, secular writers point out that Richard Nixon was a born loser and that he continually acted as such. . . . Nixon's true fault was that he had no way to plan for failure, no way to externalize his evil.[1]

Externalize—that is essential to any kind of help beyond ourselves. The minister represents that to which we reach out, not in himself or herself alone but in the very faith for which the minister stands.

In many ways this symbolic role places one in a precarious position. It seems to give the minister a special status. It is not meant to do so, for any person of faith represents that kind of resource beyond ourselves. However, in pastoral practice the representative nature of the pastor is a resource surprising in its effect. Again and again, the pastor goes to a home where there is distress, asking what can be done, only to discover that so much more is done than can be explained. Somehow presence has been a ministry in itself.

Over the years one never loses the surprise at what presence means. For a number of weeks I sat at a bedside every day or so even when the person's illness had become so exhausting that there wasn't energy for conversation. Yet it seemed important to sit often at that bedside even when the only response was the tightening of a hand at the close of a prayer. By no stretch of the imagination could it be assumed that whatever help was imparted came simply because someone sat at the bedside. I am persuaded that it was the mediation of God's presence which provided the real help.

Or again there was the time when a man went through a long mental illness, the mark of which was an almost complete withdrawal and an inaccessibility to those who wanted to reach him. Yet it did seem important to keep going to the hospital and reaching out as far as possible to the one who was inaccessible in his illness. To be sure, there were times when one could ask whether it really did any good. Did he even know that the pastor was there? Yet when recovery finally came, and we talked about the whole experience, he made clear that he knew that his pastor was there and rather depended upon it, even when he was not able to break out of his own imprisonment.

It is a common experience to discover that a pastoral call really begins at the point of the closing prayer. At that point the superficial talk is set aside, the sacramental small talk that makes up a part of any visit, and the relationship moves on to a deeper level. In that moment of prayer, however brief, the pastoral relationship is affirmed. Here is the hope for mediation, the standing together before God, the searching for the "More on which we get on board." A pastor will learn not to hurry away immediately after the prayer but to stay a moment to see if it proves to be not a closing prayer put an opening one. Often the real anxieties, the real needs, and the real hopes emerge at the time of prayer. Here the call becomes really pastoral.

3. Seeing the Whole Person

It is an obvious truth that those who seek to help persons increasingly become specialists in one aspect of the human experience. The specialties are not only the roles of physician, psychiatrist, social worker, and counselor. Within each of these categories there are further specializations. The process is probably unavoidable because of the knowledge explosion of these recent years. No one is able to handle so much knowledge even in one field.

In the face of this fact, in both the realm of therapy and development, it is easy for any person needing help to feel like a jigsaw puzzle, waiting to be put together.

In such a time when specialization has flourished so markedly, it often is natural to assume that pastors are also specialists dealing with their own thing, specifically with "spiritual resources."

My point here is that the distinction of pastors is that they are *not* specialists. The problem pastors sometimes feel in their calling, namely its general and nonspecific approach, in another sense becomes its strength. Someone needs to get it all together. Pastors who are concerned have a chance to see the whole person: the relationship to the family, the way a person feels about self, the relation to others in the church, often the feeling about one's daily work. The significance of these several factors cannot be seen until they are set down together, viewed as a whole. Thus specialization, while necessary and productive, rather than eliminating the need for the generalist, makes it even more important.

It is interesting to note that one important school of psychological thought gives strong support to the wholistic approach to understanding human problems. Gestalt psychology, beginning as a theory of perception, has broadened its approach to many areas, especially education and the theories of learning. Its essential premise, that perception takes place in configurations or gestalten, has wide implications for understanding much human behavior. In the gestalt position, we do not comprehend reality by adding up the sum total of separate parts. We learn the meaning of the part by perceiving the whole—the configuration. While this obviously is a simplistic statement, it has implications for those of us who seek to understand and support another.

In this sense, the fact that the pastor is not a specialist in the precise meaning of the word is a marked advantage. The more overall approach accepted and developed by the pastor gives insights not available elsewhere.

4. The Community of Faith

Another distinctive resource of the pastor is the church itself. The pastor does not have a clientele but is related to a community. This becomes a resource of impressive dimension when one wants to help persons.

The benefits of that community relationship are several. For one thing, it enables the pastor to be aware of emerging needs. In normal contacts one may see the signs of incipient problems. One has relationship with a person even before the problem comes to a crisis stage. In a similar way, when crisis has passed and life must pick up its rhythm again, the community of the church becomes a significant resource for assisting in that transition.

More specifically, in recent years the church has developed a particular ministry of special support groups. Within the community of faith there are clusters of those who have similar needs. The group may consist of those passing through the experiences of separation and divorce. It may be a group for women who are seeking to support one another and to understand new roles which are opening to them. In some cases it is a parent group seeking to understand the phenomenon of adolescence, and supporting one another in that important transition period. A movement presently in an early stage, but giving promise for the future, brings together groups to share ways of bringing Christian influence into the institutions in which members do their daily work. All these group relationships mean that the pastor has a distinctive, even unique, resource in the very community of faith in which he or she lives and works.

In this secular day, with its inevitable impersonalization of life, the community of faith takes on a particular significance. This is illustrated by a contrast which came in my own ministry. In the first church I served as a student, I suggested to our board of deacons that we take a survey of the village and the area around. They agreed that would be a good idea. A Sunday or so later the senior deacon suggested I come by his home that afternoon and we would talk about the survey. When I arrived, I was greeted by the aroma of coffee and the sight of an apple pie on the dining table! He suggested that we sit at the table while we had our pie and coffee and talked about the survey. He handed me paper and pencil. Then in his own mind he went down each road around the village telling me who lived where, who married whom, and any general information which might be helpful in understanding our constituency. We rounded out the whole matter that afternoon seated at his dining room table!

I had occasion to remember that when in subsequent years we decided to survey a hundred blocks around our church in Los Angeles. We organized teams, had preparatory sessions on the techniques of surveying, then went to the apartment houses and homes around us. Often we would make our way to the top floor of an apartment building only to find ourselves ringing doorbells and receiving the coolest of receptions. Often the door would open to the length of the chain, and a gruff voice would demand to know what we wanted. Usually tenants did not know the names of the people in the next apartment. This experience illustrated graphically that proximity does not make for community. It also reenforced the conviction that what the church offered in terms of community was needed even more by the people in the vast impersonal city.

It is significant that those with a thoroughly secular approach who seek to help persons have come to value the support group. In therapy where there has been no community, a small group often is organized. Yet the pastor has had that community as an intrinsic part of the ministry.

Of course, the community has to be redemptive in its nature, open to those who are in need, given to support and healing. The church is potentially a community of healing. But a pastoral concern and education are often needed to help the church find this role and not be afraid of it.

5. The Good Word

While we have many ways of saying it, "preacher of the Gospel" or "servant of the Word," the fact is that the minister is identified with a particular Good News. We are identified with a word about life which is essentially hopeful, supportive, and fulfilling. Even though one cannot fully articulate that word, the identification is important. It is a word people want to hear and believe, especially in times of trouble or transition. To be a preacher of that word is to take on an identity which people seek when need emerges.

To be sure, some preaching makes the word seem to be more judgmental than emancipating. It is possible to preach in such a way as to add new burdens to burdened people. But that, of course, is not the Good News at all. To the contrary, to share the word that "beneath are the everlasting arms" and "neither death, nor life . . . shall separate us from the love of God" is to add a special dimension to the ministry of helping persons.

It is a word which life itself does not bring forth. Many human experiences seem to deny that note of hope, and many people find it easy to despair. For us, as for the ancient world, the gospel often seems to be a scandal, a stumbling block, and foolishness in view of the "facts of life." But it often is the turning point for someone growing increasingly desperate in grappling with some problem or demand.

We need to be reminded in a secular culture that belief still is the most powerful force in human experience. In a carefully measured statement, it can be said that no power is quite equal to it. Jesus stated it in terms of stark contrast—faith as large as a mustard seed can move a mountain. It is confirmed again and again that what one believes becomes a determining factor in one's life. If the word with which the pastor is identified is a word of hope, the promise of sufficiency, and the assurance of meaning, it is a priceless gift to share.

Leslie Weatherhead tells about a man in Britain who in his mature years came to a knowledge of the gospel in his own life. At a desperate time in his life it had been the turning point for him. Impressed by the word which had saved him, he called together a group of clergymen in Britain and said, "You have the greatest news in the world. But you're not getting it across."

GETTING IT ALL TOGETHER

Throughout this chapter two hopes have given impetus to our thought. The first is that there may be a reaffirmation, or, if necessary, a recovery of respect for the pastoral resources. It is sheer loss to all when such resources go unrecognized and, therefore, unused. To covet what others bring from scientific assumptions is both futile and tragic—futile because from faith assumptions we cannot come out with scientific procedures, and tragic because we deprive persons of the very special gifts of pastoral care. The pastor must be the first to see this.

The second hope of this chapter is to show that these particular resources are strengthened and enriched when they are brought together in a combination which can be called "the pastoral." To bring into one calling the five special resources—the assumption of trust, the support of a parish community, the attempt to see life as a whole, the ministry of presence, and the good word—is to have something more than the sum total of the five. As a musical chord is more than all of its notes sounded singly, so these brought together in a calling known as pastoral have a new significance and effectiveness.

To respect these resources, to recognize that they are tested by generations of faithful practice, to see that they are especially needed for the sake of persons in a secular culture, and to seek to add new dimension and dignity to the pastoral office is a task urgently upon us. We who are pastors have the most to gain and to give by such understanding.

Chapter 4

Preaching
as Pastoral Care

As the hymn is sung before the sermon, a sensitive pastor may look over the congregation and, in the light of day-by-day pastoral care, see a great diversity of needs.

He surely will see the family where teenage rebellion is in full swing. There will be marriages known to be in trouble. There will be families where the concern for aging parents on the one hand and for growing children on the other has put a middle-aged couple under real stress.

Also, given the human condition, there will be varying degrees of emotional and mental disturbance. Others will have found themselves in some form of moral compromise, feeling under judgment but not sure how to reverse themselves. Always there will be the doubts which come at times in even the most self-sufficient life.

In a day of stress and change, there also will be men and women carrying heavy responsibilities for our institutions or committed to causes which are having a hard time of it. The faith to see them through social struggle is essential to their self-esteem, even their survival.

So the preacher, instructed by the pastoral role, may wonder how any word preached could address such a diversity of needs. Our question then becomes a specific one: What part does preaching play in pastoral care? To be sure, preaching has several roles, not one. There are great hours when it needs to be prophetic. There are times when it has a teaching function, a part of the education of the church, helping people come to an understanding of the historic faith. There are other times when the need to undergird the community of faith requires preaching to be promotional and persuasive. But in the midst of all these, there is an historic and respected role of the pulpit in extending pastoral care to those in the congregation.

But how can that care be given through the pulpit? In the minister there is a combination of roles not found anywhere else, to my knowledge. It is the attempt to bring together the private role of the pastor and the public role of the preacher. Can that really be done? Can preaching really be pastoral?

POSSIBLE NEGATIVE EFFECTS OF PREACHING

Many of those deeply involved in pastoral practice have genuine reservations about the place of preaching. To them it seems contrary to the very conditions that make for good pastoral care.

Some feel that the preaching situation assumes a form of authority which weakens and even negates a good pastoral relation. To mount the pulpit which is notably "six feet above contradiction" is in itself a reversal of the relation a pastor ought to have, especially to persons in real need. The role of the pastor easily becomes, either really or apparently, authoritarian. Such a relationship carried over into pastoral care works against the comfort and acceptance which the pastoral relationship requires.

Often, say the critics, preaching works against pastoral principles. It becomes, for one thing, guilt producing. It sets up impossible standards and adds guilt to those already guilt-ridden. Or, on the other side of it, it may offer a false and easy solution. People often identify with the problem with which the preacher is dealing, when theirs is quite different. Thus they are diverted from facing the reality of their own needs.

Added to these is the possibility that preaching may raise questions about the confidentiality of the pastor. It's so easy for the preacher directly or indirectly to make reference to conversations or situations which illustrate the point of the sermon! Since the person needing counsel is usually supersensitive, the very fact that the preacher will be speaking publicly raises real inhibitions. As we already have noted, sometimes preachers mistakenly feel that if they refer to someone's coming to talk with them, others will be encouraged to do so. To the contrary, such allusions usually have a reverse effect. Confidentiality is too essential to good pastoral practice to be threatened by any preaching practice.

These are criticisms to be faced honestly. In my judgment, none of these negative effects is intrinsic to preaching itself. To be sure, in the hands of an authoritarian person, preaching becomes a ready instrument of domination; it is particularly open to this abuse. But the same person who will abuse the preaching office is likely to use the other relationships in the same way, whether in the counseling room, the hospital, the home, or the committee room. The problem lies with the preacher, not with preaching itself.

PASTORAL PREACHING

Believing that the positive aspects of the preaching office far outweigh the negations, let us consider the distinctive contributions which preaching makes to pastoral care. To those who recognize these gifts and learn the skills that go with them, preaching becomes a fine instrument for helping people. From their pulpits there can come four discernible gifts which support pastoral care: disclosure, insight, the word of hope, and sacrament.

1. Disclosure

Preachers often underestimate the degree to which they make themselves known in their preaching. People who hear the preacher bring the word Sunday by Sunday have a feeling of relationship to him or her. The preaching experience discloses the preacher as person. Those who hear begin to sense whether the pastor is a caring person, open and concerned. It is a strange truth that often the preacher speaks of intimate feelings and experiences more easily in the pulpit than in more direct conversation. C. C. Morrison used to call that "the public privacy of the pulpit." By this he meant that we speak of things deep in our lives. In that speaking, we disclose something of ourselves.

Translated into pastoral care, this means that an initial relationship already has come about through the preaching office. Ministers are sometimes surprised to learn how they are "known," a truth which confirms that the preaching relationship is really very personal.

Of all the qualities disclosed in the preacher none is as supportive of pastoral care as Christian love, what the New Testament calls "agape." In this regard, it is especially unfortunate that First Corinthians has been divided into chapters! The chapters separate what was not meant to be separated. It is easy to conclude that the twelfth chapter of First Corinthians is dealing with gifts within the church and the thirteenth is dealing with a general quality called love. In fact, when Paul wrote the section we call the thirteenth chapter, he still was talking about gifts within the church. He spoke of the variety of gifts: of utterance of wisdom, of knowledge, of gifts of healing, or working of miracles, of gifts of tongues and interpretation of tongues. He acknowledged these as great gifts to be used within the church.

But having listed them, he went on to write, "I will show you a still more excellent way," and from this moved on directly to talk about the meaning of love. What must not be lost is the truth that this is still a gift within the church. "The greatest of these is love."

Among the ways in which that love is manifest is the time of preaching. It has a way of making itself known in the word, the manner, and the spirit of the preacher. Where that is disclosed, we may be sure that it has given tremendous support to the pastoral care within that fellowship.

It has to be said in equal honesty that those things which inhibit the pastoral relationship also show up, often without our being aware of it. Here can be seen the kind of hostility, or immaturity, or special pleading which closes the door to genuine pastoral care. One way or another, preaching *is* a time of disclosure, not only of the truth, but also of the person presenting the truth. That is why the pulpit cannot be separated from the other means of grace so important to the care of persons. At no point does the admonition come closer home, "Let love be genuine." The pulpit is one place where you cannot get away very long with the counterfeit!

George Matheson is best known for his hymn "O, Love That Will Not Let Me Go." Most of his ministry was in a poor district in Edinburgh where Sunday by Sunday he preached to the working people of the area. When the time came to close his ministry, Matheson said, "My sermons may have flown over your heads like the bird of Paradise; but my life has been level with your own. . . ."[1] There could be no doubt in the minds of those who heard that in him also was a love which would not let them go! It is a priceless ingredient in the pulpit. When such love is disclosed, we turn toward it as hungry men and women turn toward nourishment. Here the pulpit is a superb means of grace.

2. Insight

Another quality of pastoral preaching is insight. It often takes people by surprise to hear the preacher give evidence that she or he understands what is going on in another's life. It is that quality which caused a member of the congregation listening to John Wesley to say, "This man understands the deepest secrets of my heart." In that startling discovery the healing often already has started.

It is a life-changing encounter to discover that we are known. The theme of "being known" runs constantly through the biblical Word. When the prophet speaks of the day when every man shall know God, the real meaning is "shall know that he is known." So Paul promises that one day we shall know even as now we "are known." The discovery that someone understands and shares the experience which is deep in us is an immeasurable support for the pastoral relation that can come about through preaching. There are those occasions when the worshiper is startled to discover that the preacher is really addressing the need supposedly hidden. Any preaching that can do that has set into motion the redemptive forces of the gospel. Life can never be quite the same when we discover that we are already known!

It is at this point that the preaching loses its dullness and takes on life. It is futile to try to find gimmicks to add interest to a sermon. Interest comes by involvement. Whenever it becomes apparent that the preacher is addressing our real needs, interest follows inevitably. All of us are interested in that which addresses our own lives.

After a radio broadcast in which I referred to Washington Gladden, the mail brought a letter sharing a personal incident. The name of Dr. Gladden had touched a cherished memory in one of the listeners. He wrote that he had been in Columbus, Ohio, as a young man intending to study art. Walking down Broad Street, he had seen people going into the First Congregational Church. Strangely attracted by the crowd, he had followed and taken a place on the back pew. For him this brought an unexpected turn of events. A member of a conservative Baptist congregation, he had never been in a church other than Baptist!

When Washington Gladden preached, the young man found himself strangely addressed. The preacher was speaking to some hopes the young man barely had faced in himself.

At the close of the service Dr. Gladden remained in the front of the sanctuary, and those who wished to greet him went forward. The shy young man moved forward, strangely drawn to the preacher. In the front of the church, however, his shyness overcame him and he stood back. Dr. Gladden saw him, left the group with whom he was shaking hands, and spoke to the young man. Surprisingly he asked the visitor's name and invited him to come to his study the next evening at seven.

In that encounter the next evening the young man's life changed direction. The hopes the sermon had addressed came to the front, and the young man moved into the Christian ministry. At the time of the writing he had given a lifetime ministry on university campuses. All those years later, he could not forget the occasion when unexpectedly he had found himself addressed at a deep level by someone who understood the hopes of a young man.

Many of us could speak of similar occasions. They are times we will not forget. It was as though the Good News came with our name on it. When that kind of understanding is in the preacher, there is no doubt about the pastoral care it provides.

This is one reason, of course, we who preach always must stand at the intersection where the gospel crosses our own time. To be sure, human experience is timeless, but it always has its timely aspects. And pastoral preaching must understand the contemporary as well as the eternal. To stand at that intersection, to gain insight into the feelings, the frustrations, the anxieties, and the aspirations of a particular generation is to find in the pulpit an occasion of real and saving encounter.

3. The Word of Hope

In the great diversity of need which we already have noted, there is one thing held in common: the need for hope. Sometimes that hope is very specific. It is for an improvement of health, a change of circumstance, the healing of a relationship, or any one of the urgencies which mark the human condition.

Sometimes the need for hope is far more general, and also more pervasive. There is a nameless hopelessness that comes at some times in life, and it lays a heavy burden upon any who have it. It depletes the energies, paralyzes many of our abilities, and leaves us unhappy, sometimes to the extreme. So one may be sure that in any congregation the need of hope, specific or general, is shared by most.

The discovery of that hope is often the difference between victory and defeat, even life and death. When hope is found, men and women rise incredibly above difficult circumstances. Without hope even a modest testing may prove to be too much for a person to bear. Sometimes it is not understood that hope is a *given*. By that we mean that it usually has to come from *outside*. If hope could be generated from inside ourselves, we certainly would do it at earliest opportunity. To be without hope is too painful to endure any longer than we have to. But in the nature of our experience, hope comes from receiving a new word, usually some new factor that changes the picture. It is that word which the preacher seeks to bring from the pulpit. If that hope can be imparted, pastoral care of the highest order takes place. The word from the pulpit can be the turning point which makes more intimate pastoral care possible.

In the drama based upon the moving *Diary of Anne Frank* there is a memorable scene which illustrates this point. For months a group of Jewish people have been in hiding in the attic of a Dutch home. They have been sheltered from the Nazi persecution and living so closely together with meager food and cramped quarters that it has brought many tensions. One night these pent-up feelings come out when one man sneaks from his bed and tries to get a little extra food. He is discovered by the mother of small children. Angered, she berates him loudly. She finally tells him to get out, that she does not want to see him again. This arouses the whole household, and the latent hostilities begin to come out one by one.

In the midst of this there is a knock at the door. Such a sound brings its own terror. They wait to see if the knock gives the friendly signal. When it does, they open the door and a young Dutch girl moves quickly inside and closes the door. Standing in the middle of the room she says, "I have news! I have news! Something has happened! The invasion has begun."

The invasion! That hour for which they had waited so long, the evidence that at last help was coming from outside! When the word first comes, there is a moment of stunned silence, as though it is too much to take in all at once. Then there follows a kind of celebration, a release of all the pent-up tensions. After some moments of this, they begin to turn to one another to embrace, to ask forgiveness, to seek reconciliation.

What had made the difference? They still were prisoners in the attic. The release had not yet come. But something else had come—a word of hope. It was the hope that transformed the situation. They could not generate it within themselves. It had to come from outside. It was a given.

In many ways this is a parable of the gospel. The Word brought in the midst of many limiting human situations is that God's invasion of human life has come in Jesus Christ. The preacher's responsibility is to translate that hope into the specific situations in which people often struggle or feel themselves imprisoned.

To make that hope clear is to give pastoral care, to begin the liberation, to provide the setting in which one can be pastor as well as preacher. As long as there is such a word of hope to proclaim, the pulpit need not question whether it has a role in the pastoral care of persons.

4. Sacrament

This brings us to the distinctive affirmation about preaching which marks our faith, namely, that it is a time when we expect God's action over and above our own. Mystery though it is—and admittedly a foolishness in many minds—this belief about preaching is deeply rooted. Preaching is not just public address. It is not only teaching or counseling or admonition. It is sacramental, in the sense in which sacrament is defined by the Anglican catechism as "an outward and visible sign of an inward and spiritual grace given unto us . . . as a means whereby to receive this grace."

Of course that seems foolishness indeed to those who never have affirmed the basic belief from which it is derived, namely, that God has willed to disclose himself to us and actively seeks to find opening into our lives. But by preaching? It seems so "ordinary" for such hope! Yet the nature of sacrament is to take ordinary things and make them means of grace, "the signs of God's address," as Buber put it. A faith which affirms that bread and cup can become means of God's grace surely can believe that words preached in faith and heard in faith CAN be sacramental.

CAN be, but ARE they? We think of all the dull pedestrian sermons we have heard, and we wonder if such audacious belief in preaching may not be merely delusion. Can such preaching as we commonly hear really impart grace to those who are in need of pastoral support and care?

To say that preaching can be sacramental is not to release us from human effort of the highest order. To prepare for a sacramental experience requires more, not less, preparation. The promise of grace is not an indulgence for careless preparation. It takes a faithful discipline to be able to say of preaching what Paul wrote to the

Galatians, "I do not frustrate the grace of God . . ." (2:21, KJV). But many of our sermons must do just that!

CHECKPOINTS FOR AN EFFECTIVE SERMON

Because of the importance of the pastoral sermon when seen in the light of people in need, it becomes even more urgent to do everything possible to make the sermon a fitting means of communication. What a loss it is to all when the word does not get through, largely because the preacher has never learned, or having learned is neglecting his or her craftsmanship! Pastoral preaching, as a well-known advertisement says, is "when you care enough to send the very best."

Yet many of our sermons fall short of helping because we have not taken into account some of the basic simplicities of communication. Often a sermon falls short not because the preacher is not concerned, nor because the word is not true, but because the sermon has not been put into a form which can be understood.

Shortly after the Korean War, I went out on a preaching mission to the air bases in Korea and Japan. To a civilian like myself this was full of new experiences. One of these was sitting in the cockpit beside the pilot on occasional flights. Full of questions, I asked one day about a listing of fifteen items on a metal plate above the instruments, in full view of the pilot. "That," he said, "is the checklist. Regulations require us to check every one of those fifteen items before we take off." "Every time?" I asked. "Every time." He left no doubt about it.

That was almost twenty-five years ago, and ever since then I've had a checklist of my own for a sermon! It's not ready to fly until at least five things have been checked out!

1. What Do You Want to Say?

The answer to that has to come to a focal point. What's the *main* thing you intend to say around which all else must find its supportive place? If it can't be stated in a sentence or two, the sermon probably is not ready to go!

2. To Whom Do You Want to Say It?

What need in human life are you addressing? If you know your subject, do you know your object? A real sermon is not for general distribution, like fourth-class mail, addressed "Occupant" or "Pewholder." It's personally addressed in terms of defined needs, known and understood by the preacher, and in due time, by the listener, too.

3. How Do You Feel About This Matter?

This moves into the whole area of our nonverbal communication. Our feelings come through even when we don't know it! We may even be in the position of saying angrily, "Didn't I tell you to love one another!" Every preacher must come to terms with the feeling tone of what is said, for hostility or frustration or even boredom may come through far more than the words spoken.

4. What Response Do You Expect?

This does not mean that every sermon requires explicit action. The purpose may be confirmation of truth already known, remembering that "those who know it best seem hungering and thirsting to hear it like the rest." Or the purpose of the sermon may be reversal or awareness or imparting a sense of belonging to those who hear. But the preacher ought to know, and then help the listener to know, what response is expected and prayed for.

5. What's the Good News in This Sermon?

Yes, every Christian sermon ought to have that note, even if it's the hard news of God's judgment. For the Good News has many sides— comfort in our sorrow, hope in our despair, joy in our boredom, justice when we are wronged, claim when we feel useless. In some way, every sermon should reflect that we are preachers of the *gospel*.

Preaching IS a lifelong discipline, a way of life, a total commitment. But great intent does not release us from asking the workaday basic questions of craftsmanship. We have no right to let neglected disciplines bring forth a sermon which "frustrates the grace of God."

Chapter 5

Helping People in Times of Crisis

When trouble comes, where do people turn for help? There is no one answer, of course. It may be to a friend, or to a physician, or to any one of the growing number of counseling centers. But to the surprise of some, studies consistently show that more people think first of the pastor than of any other single category. To be sure, this first contact often leads to referral. But the pastor is the one to whom many turn first in the time of crisis.

A number of things contribute to this. Often the pastor seems to be more available and less expensive! There usually has been previous even continuous contact before the crisis situation arises. Also, the very term "pastor" often is associated with times of extremity. We assume a pastor is there for times of trouble.

The question then is not whether the pastor will deal with personal crises, but how, for it is a special skill. No discussion of an authentic pastoral ministry, therefore, can avoid very serious thought about the ways which help, and those which don't.

THE REAL NATURE OF CRISIS

We need, first of all, to understand what a crisis is. It is more than a disrupted situation or a time of stress, intense as these may be.

A crisis is a time when one's whole life seems to be threatened. In some degree, the things we value most seem hanging in the balance. Or more deeply, our very sense of self seems under attack. The meaning of a life may be at stake.

Ernest Hemingway, speaking of writing, once observed, "The worst death for anyone is to lose the center of his being, the thing he really is." It is that center, whatever it may be, which seems threatened when crisis comes. That's why crisis brings anxiety and urgency. The problem which has created the crisis immediately moves to top priority. All emergency signals of a life flash on. Nothing is as important as seeing that crisis through. Often all else is held in abeyance.

Psychologically, crisis is the time when we feel that the wholeness of life is about to be broken, the wholeness which gives life its meaning. In gestalt psychology, we are reminded that each of us has a "configuration" which gives us some sense of who we are and how we are related to our world. We see ourselves in relationship to other people, to ourselves, to the work we have to do, to the values we cherish. When crisis comes, that configuration is threatened. If it really is broken, then we go through an anguished time when life loses its meaning and security. It really seems a life or death matter, with time running out.

The feel of crisis may be illustrated by a boyhood experience. One summer my brother and I were out in a boat on the river. I decided to jump overboard and swim to shore. After I had gone for some time, I became aware that I either had underestimated the distance or had overestimated my strength! Though the years have been many, I still can recall swimming on, but stopping periodically to put my foot down to see if I was near enough to stand on solid bottom. Failing to find a place to stand, there was no choice but to swim on, wondering with mounting panic whether my strength would last. In many ways that is the feel of crisis. You can even find a text for it in the Sixty-ninth Psalm, "Save me, O God! For the waters have come up to my neck . . . where there is no foothold"!

The most salient mark of crisis then is anxiety. The pastor learns that this anxiety has a particular focus. In many ways what we fear most is not pain or adversity, but what these will do to us. Our anxiety is not whether the adversity will come, but whether we will be able to take it. The basic fear is of inadequacy. What one dreads most in the crisis is the discovery that one simply will not be able to meet the occasion. That fear of insufficiency, along with the threat of brokenness, is the heart of suffering in time of crisis. What we fear most is that life will crumble at the core. We will lose our "selves." Pastoral ministry must seek to bring reassurance addressed to that central need.

COMMON CRISES

If this is the nature of crisis, then even a brief review of everyday experience will show in how many circumstances it appears. All of us know times and conditions of human life which in every sense can be called crises.

Death of a Loved One

Here the configuration of life is radically broken. There is no escape from having to readjust the whole of one's life to the loss. Dr. Kübler-Ross has rendered a real contribution in confirming that adjustment to one's own impending death passes through definite and discernible stages. In a similar way there are stages of adjustments to the death of a loved one, and the pastor needs to understand them. Those stages mark nothing less than the resolution of a crisis. At first there is a kind of merciful anesthesia against the full shock. It is as though God has given us an advance of grace to see us through the first days of our loss. There follow in succession the other stages which include times of inundating grief and despair, other times of guilt, questioning whether we did all we could to give the loved one a chance for life. There usually follows a time of recovering memories and sorting them out, until the loved one comes again to an enduring place in memory over which death no longer has dominion. Grief, then, is the process of moving back into life. It is the discovery that, in spite of all fears, life can go on. Though one cannot set the precise time of any phase, there is the assurance that the signs of healing will appear.

In many ways, seeing the crisis of bereavement all the way through is one area where pastoral care needs to be greatly improved. It is natural for the pastor to be present and supportive in the first onslaught of grief. There is the funeral service, and the consultation in preparation for it. But real pastoral care will recognize the ongoing nature of the crisis, helping the bereaved to understand the emerging stages through which grief will go. We pastors have a special ministry here, and we should be more faithful in seeing it all the way through, a private faithfulness when other friends and supporters have gone on with their lives.

A Broken Primary Relationship, Such as Separation or Divorce

Again, the center of life has been threatened. The reactions to which we referred earlier are very evident in this kind of experience: the fear of inadequacy, the sense of brokenness, the loss of meaning. While lawyers can work out legal arrangements, the deeper question is what happens to the selfhood of those involved. This inner crisis has to be faced with all the pain involved. Often it brings a shattered self-image. It has its own form of grief, the pain of something lost. It evokes all kinds of fears of the future, especially the feelings of failure and loneliness.

A special word needs to be said again about the helpfulness of groups which have been formed for those passing through the divorce or separation experience. As has been shown many times, those who have a common experience can help one another. They know the games that we play on ourselves and can expose them with compassion but realism. It may be the pastor's role to help relate the separated person to such a group. At least, no one should be expected to go through that deep, personal crisis alone.

Physical Illness

Serious illness, too, can mean the loss of the center of a life, whether it is the prospect of invalidism or of death. The practice of giving pastors access to hospitals at any hour of the day or night is the recognition of the important ministry one has in helping people face the emotional aspects of their illness as a part of the healing itself.

This seems to have enhanced importance in these days when institutions inevitably become more impersonal. Often doctors are extremely busy and do not have the time to talk with the patient, or to listen, as one sorts out the anxieties which have been evoked by the condition. Often physicians do not know how to deal with this kind of emotional need. In many ways the pastor is rendering a ministry simply by having that time to listen and by offering such reassurance as a nonmedical approach can allow. The spiritual aspects of an illness are varied indeed. Sometimes it is an anxiety not commensurate with the illness. There are also times when the very will to live seems to have been lost. Sometimes the practical aspects of adjustment of income and living conditions shadow a family.

Whichever the form of the anxiety, the pastor can help the patient deal with it, at least by listening.

Here pastors will often be frustrated by the sheer imprecision of their ministry. Our "instruments" are simply those of human relationships. One uses words, presence, the quiet reminders of faith, and times of prayer to help a patient through the crisis attendant upon illness. These tools are hard to measure or control! But they are all essential, even at times, determinative.

Far more difficult are the times of mental illness, which can become crisis in its most urgent and intense form. Here not only the patient but also those related come under great duress. Such illness can mean a readjustment not only for the patient but also for the whole family in their manner of living.

Most urgent in the time of emotional or mental illness is the sustaining of hope. When the illness takes the form of deep depression or bizarre behavior, it is easy to fall into despair. Usually the recovery from mental illness, as compared with physical illness, requires a longer span of time. There will be periods of advance and periods of seeming regression. But increasingly the prognosis for recovery is favorable. It is important that the pastor be prepared to interpret to family members something of the nature of the experience through which they are passing. Above all, that note of hope must be given with as much realism as possible.

As the patient begins the recovery from emotional or mental illness, the fellowship of the church takes on added importance. In that fellowship can be found the reentry into the normal relationships of life. Here one can hope to find compassion with a sturdy realism that knows when to stand off or to stand close. The church that has maturity and grace can be a "Bridge over Troubled Waters."

One of the difficult decisions families sometimes face is whether to take action to commit a loved one to a hospital against his or her will. This is agonizing in the extreme; yet families sometimes have to make this decision for the welfare of the one that they love. At such a time the pastor needs to be close with counsel and reassurance.

Life Work

In our culture, the work span of life may become shorter at precisely the time when life expectancy is greater. To have work terminate, by retirement or by dismissal, is often a crisis for the persons involved. Again the classic evidences of crisis can be found:

the feeling of inadequacy, the loss of meaning, and the fear of brokenness. Such a time may also bring out family stresses which were there but not explicit.

Spiritual Crises

No discussion of crises would be complete without reminder of spiritual crisis which comes in some lives. Long ago William James described the conversion process in terms which are still true, though we rarely use the language. He noted that out of a sense of crisis can come that profound change of life called conversion. He described it as ". . . the process, gradual or sudden, by which a self hitherto divided, and consciously wrong inferior and unhappy, becomes unified and consciously right superior and happy, in consequence of its firmer hold upon religious realities."[1]

Is there not evidence that this kind of crisis of spirit is appearing more and more often in our secular life? Perhaps our prototype is the rich young ruler who was "the man who had everything," yet still asked, "What do I still lack?" In his biography of Blaise Pascal, Mortimer says of him at one period:

> Even God was absent. That was the void within the void. Externally Pascal was a made man and a celebrity. . . . Inwardly he was beaten to his knees, looking every way for help but not greatly hoping for any, for who could give him what was not there to be given? And even if it were there, who of those he knew could bring it?[2]

What if that kind of crisis is stated for us in secular terms? Is it any less real? Does not God still quicken in us the need for him, in order that his gifts may be more readily received?

The sensitive pastor will be alert for signs of "God's address," as Buber put it, which are "not something extraordinary . . . they are just what goes on time and again, just what goes on in any case."[3] Augustine described his own experience in similar terms: "He who we desire to receive himself causes us to ask; he whom we wish to find himself causes us to seek; he unto whom we strive to come causes us to knock."

That is a crisis at its deepest level. It happens even to the person who has everything—except self-esteem, a sense of peace with oneself, and a sustaining meaning in life.

THE DISTINCTIONS OF PASTORAL MINISTRY

If this is the nature of crisis, and these are some of the ways by which it is seen most commonly in human experience, what is the pastor's distinctive ministry?

One of the most important aspects of this ministry is to recognize there are no stereotypes, and few precise procedures, however much we may wish for them. We are dealing with basic human relationships, with all the diversity and uncertainty which they involve. How often a pastor will not know where to turn or what to do! To that extent the pastor has entered into the experience of the very one she or he is trying to help.

It seems to me that in times of crisis the pastor has several distinctive ministries to bring. They can be summarized as: awareness, empathy, witness, referral, and absorption. They deserve our consideration.

Awareness

Few crises emerge without some warning. To be sure, there are catastrophic moments when trouble comes "like a bolt out of the blue." But more often there is a process involved, and there are premonitory signs. Some of these are very familiar. There may be withdrawal from the fellowship without any real explanation. Sometimes there may be a sudden or mounting rise in demand for time and attention. Or there may be an undue irritability or a hostility which emerges in inappropriate and unexpected ways.

Here pastors have a real advantage. For when such signs appear, we can take limited initiative by being present with one for whom we are concerned. To be sure, that option can be abused. Only rarely can one come at another's problem head-on. But there are moments of opening when the hurt that comes with crisis has prepared the way. It is deeply important to sense the crisis in its early stages before its own destructive work has begun.

Empathy

Here is one of the mysteries of human relationships. To know that someone is sharing our pain, standing by in a time of uncertainty, even sharing our anxiety has a strange comforting and healing effect. Empathy in its way is therapy. It strangely helps alleviate suffering. After these many years I can recall a way my father had of comforting one of us when some hurt had come. When we ran to him with some minor injury, a bump or a cut, often weeping with the pain, he rarely said, "Oh, come on now. That isn't much!" He never admonished, as I recall, "Big boys don't cry!" But it was not uncommon for him to stop his work, listen to the story, perhaps look at the injury and simply say, "That *really* hurts!" A strange response when you think of it. It told us nothing we did not really know. After all, it was our hurt, not his. Yet one always felt helped! It was a *response.* You knew you had been heard. Someone else was sharing the hurt with you, and that knowledge helped.

Again, showing empathy seems such an imprecise way to help people. It seems one has done nothing. But in the mystery of human relations empathy has its own healing. It lessens the loneliness. It somehow begins to break into the tragic circle of self-absorption in which hurt feeds upon itself.

Mediation

When crisis comes, we all reach out for help beyond ourselves. It is a sound instinct. While we can call up the reserves from within ourselves to meet the extra needs of crisis, there is a limit beyond which we cannot go alone. Our hope lies in finding new resources, a new relationship, a new gift, a new level of faith, even a new word.

It cannot be said too strongly that this mediation often is the pastor's major role in the crisis hours. It is to bear quiet witness to our faith that help *is* available from outside ourselves, the gift of God to those who need Him.

In his young manhood William James went through an incapacitating depression. His letters and diary reveal the anguish of those months. He confessed that "the fear was so invasive and powerful that, if I had not clung to Scripture texts ... I think I should have grown really insane." On April 30, 1870, there was an entry of marked significance in his diary. Persuaded of the power of free will in one's life, he wrote:

> Hitherto when I have felt like taking a free initiative, like daring to act originally, without carefully waiting for contemplation of the external world to determine all for me, suicide seemed the most manly form to put my daring into; now, I will go a step further with my will, not only act with it, but believe as well ... My belief, to be sure, *can't* be optimistic— but I will posit life ... Life shall [be built in] doing and suffering and creating.[4]

Three years later William James's father wrote about his son:

> He came in the other afternoon while I was sitting alone, and after walking the floor in an animated way for a moment, broke out, "Bless my soul, what a difference between me as I am now and as I was last

spring at this time . . . now with my mind so cleared up and restored to sanity. It's the difference between life and death."[5]

To understand this experience, it needs to be seen that the turning point was not merely a resolution on James's part. It was a response to new truth which had come to him. "I think that yesterday was a crisis in my life. I finished the first part of Renouvier's second 'Essais' and see no reason why his definition of Free Will . . . need be the definition of an illusion."[6] That new possibility was the turning point. Something new had been added. In James's case it was a new idea. But it may be a new relationship, a new sense of forgiveness, an understanding, and most of all, a new moment of faith. Resolution of personal crisis begins when something new comes into the picture.

Once aware of this process, the pastor will look for that moment when that inbreaking can come. The hope in a time of crisis, then, is for a form of "advent." Something comes into a life which is given from outside—a grace, an assurance, an understanding. Usually it comes by mediation from someone who has responded to another's need, as Peter responded to the needy man at the temple, "I have no silver and gold, but I give you what I have; in the name of Jesus Christ of Nazareth, walk" (Acts 3:6).

The pastor will have many occasions to remember this scene. We often seem unable to give what others want of us. But we can add, "I give you what I have." Often one is astonished to see how much is mediated over and above the little we seem to bring to the situation. Both the readiness to receive and the willingness to give are a part of God's healing work in human life.

In my judgment, pastors need to use the language of faith more boldly. To be sure, such language has been misused, causing us to shy away from a misplaced piety. But in the pastoral process there come moments when those words *can* be spoken with naturalness and reality. They may be the most distinctive gift a pastor can bring to the time of crisis. At the right moments those words mediate faith.

Referral

One of the advantages of the secular day is the great proliferation of human services: The pastor needs to be in touch with those in the community who can bring special help—the social worker, the psychiatrist, the marriage counselor. To be alert to the indications that referral is advisable will be a part of sound pastoral practice.

But when is it indicated? Generally, if a person is to be helped by the pastoral approach, a certain measure of wholeness in that person is required. The pastor will need to be alert to signs of mental or emotional pathology. Where this seems a possibility, psychiatric consultation should be sought.

One learns to look for certain signs. *Excessiveness* is one of them. Many neurotic attitudes are normal ones in exaggeration! Excessive dependence, excessive hostility, excessive piety, or excessive activity are signs which ought to be taken into account. Another is the *apparent loss of touch with reality.* When it is suspected that the one in crisis is having difficulty distinguishing between reality and unreality, help should be sought immediately. *Loss of autonomy* is another. None of us is completely autonomous, of course. We all can say with Paul, "For I do not do what I want, but I do the very thing I hate" (Romans 7:15). That's part of human experience. But when actions seem unduly compulsive even to the point of being bizarre, then some psychiatric consultation is imperative.

Because of the great diversity of views in psychiatry itself, the pastor will need to conduct some inquiry to find a colleague whose approach is congenial to pastoral practice. Consulting with physicians in one's own congregation may help in getting a recommendation. Also, other pastors more familiar with the medical community may be helpful when one begins a new pastorate. One way or another, finding such a psychiatric colleague is genuinely important. When the relationship has been established, it often becomes mutually supportive: the pastor as one who sees illness in its incipient stages, the psychiatrist as one who brings special medical skills for particular ills.

Not all referrals are psychiatric, of course. The needs for special help touch every aspect of human experience: social work, financial counsel, legal aid, psychological testing, and marriage clinics, to mention a few. But the pastor who would help in crisis must be at home in that confidential caring network.

Absorption

Many feelings will be directed toward any pastor who gets involved in a crisis situation. Some of those feelings will be surprising, and often seemingly inappropriate. There may be unexpected and sudden angers. There may be withdrawal, a retreat into reserve or even silence. Sometimes it is a reversion to a kind of childlike dependence when someone seems to say, "I'm going to let you decide it. I'll do what you tell me." The pastor will know that these are the surface signs of an inner crisis. They are the reaction to stress. One will need to absorb these with maturity, accepting them for what they are, outward signs of inward conflict, and not be diverted into dealing with symptoms alone. Above all, it is essential not to be drawn into defensiveness. When that happens, the pastoral role has been lost. This, in part, is what is meant by absorption.

One of these reactions which may baffle the pastor, or even bring hurt, is the evidence of rejection after the crisis is past. To be with a person in crisis may make for a relationship on a deeper and firmer basis. But not always. Sometimes when the crisis has been resolved to manageable levels, the person helped will feel the need to put behind him or her the whole experience, including those who have shared it. To some degree, the sufferer may feel a loss of face, a disclosure of weakness which would not have happened if the pain had not become so intense. When the crisis is past, there may be the need to close and seal that chapter as fully as possible. That may include rejecting the very relationships which were most helpful in the crisis period. That rejection may come as a quiet setting of distance, a seeming withdrawal, made even more evident by the fact that it follows the time of unusual closeness. The pastor must accept this as part of the process, not without sadness, but as far as possible, without hurt. It may be the sign not that pastoral care has failed, but that it has been effective.

CRISIS AND NEWNESS OF LIFE

This, then, is the ministry in times of crisis. It is ministry in its most redemptive form. In a strange way, crises may lead into our greatest fulfillment. To be sure, there are crises which are sheer tragedy, with no good coming from them which human wisdom can perceive. Even so, the deepest things in our lives, those which we cherish most, often come out of crises faced and transcended. No one can say whether that's why crisis comes in human life. In many ways every crisis evokes two questions: Where did it come from? What is to come of it?

Fritz Kunkel, from a lifetime of counseling, spoke of the positive gifts which inner crisis leaves behind:

> This drastic experience we call the major crisis. All egocentricity leads toward it. Moreover, it should be welcomed; for through its suffering, as will be seen, we may move into that joy and peace which comes from

releasing the Self within from the limitations of its shell into the creative, productive, courageous, loving expressions of which it is capable. That is indeed the abundant life.[7]

True pastoral care seeks to further that resolution.

Chapter 6

Ministry in
the Life Cycle

By the nature of the calling, the minister often is with people on those occasions which mark the transitions in their lives. Traditional ceremonies of the church have grown up around these very times. Baptism or dedication of infants, baptism or confirmation at adolescence, graduations, weddings, retirements, memorial services—all are considered normal parts of the work of the minister.

These also are the times when life is most real for us all. By an unstudied instinct these are hours when we sense both the mystery and the meaning of life. Ceremony gives us a chance to reach out in celebration and commitment.

A recent Thanksgiving service in our church ended with a Procession of Life. Down the center aisle came those representing stages of life's unfolding. In steady procession they came: two preschool children, a preteenager, a teenager, a college-age youth, a single adult, a couple, a family, an older couple whose children had grown, and finally a ninety-two-year-old widow. Each stopped for a moment before the altar and gave thanks for God's gifts at that stage of life. For those of us who saw it, the experience was deeply moving. In a matter of moments there unfolded the psalmist's faith, "Surely goodness and mercy shall follow me all the days of my life."

When the emotional impact had subsided, however, we realized that the progression of life rarely moves so smoothly. There are detours and obstructions and rough places along the way. Especially at each time of entry into a new phase of our lives there are difficult decisions, resistances, and often emotional turmoil. As equinoctial storms mark the change of seasons, so life seems to have its marked instabilities in the transition times. There may be a feeling of resistance; one wants to go backward instead of forward. Because of uncertainty, one may try to prolong the present which is known and postpone the future which is unknown. Some even are tempted to say, "Stop the cycle. I want to get off!"

To see through these inescapable changes and, at the same time, adjust to those whom we love who are experiencing changes in their lives is a constant and demanding part of being a human being. It *is* the life story. As much as we would like to have assurance, there is no built-in guarantee of a happy ending. The risks of passage are real.

INSIDE THE LIFE CYCLE

The pastor who ministers in the secular setting has some real advantages, for significant studies of the life cycle have been made, and they give us helpful insights. One book entitled *Passages: The Predictable Crises of Adult Life* became a best seller in a short time. Earlier than this, the more scientific work of Eric Erickson not only delineated the progressive stages of life but also described the emotional tone of each.

It is of particular interest to us to note that Erickson found conflict in every stage of life. From the beginning of life to its end, we are engaged in inner struggle, each stage having its own.

For example, according to Erickson, even the infant is struggling between trust and mistrust. For the small child the conflict is autonomy versus shame and doubt. For the older child it is between initiative and guilt. So through eight stages of life, conflict continues: industry versus inferiority, identity versus identity confusion, intimacy versus isolation, and, in full maturity, generativity versus stagnation. The eighth and final stage in Erickson's scheme is still struggle, by that time between integrity and despair.

Such a study raises the question: Is the term "life cycle" really descriptive? It may be, in the sense that the stages of life reappear in each person. But "cycle" is not descriptive of the unfolding experience within the individual person. It is not a cycle in the sense of coming back to where it began! It is progression, marked by struggle, allowing no turning back, subject to many variations, and ending in the radical, ultimate experience of death. That's not a cycle!

BASIC MARKS OF LIFE'S PROGRESSION

Several characteristics of this progression need to be kept in mind by the pastor who stays close to reality in being with people:

First, any new stage of maturity is marked not by the *resolution* of inner conflict, but by *change* of it. To live is to know conflict. Health is not the absence of struggle but the progression within it. However much we may long for it, there is no honorable discharge along the way.

Second, in that progression we know that we are the moved, not the movers. We do not set the time clock nor can we really stop it. But our lives are not automated by the very scheme of things. Human freedom finds lots of room within the limits that cannot be changed. But we do have to find that freedom within those terms.

Third, each transition requires a new act of faith. We enter each phase of life like Abraham, who went out not knowing where he was to go. We see the changes in circumstances and relationships in the life cycle. We often do not sense the inner leap of faith each transition requires.

A homely figure of speech comes from memories of the circus! One thinks of the aerialists who perform such feats of daring, none more than the one who goes flying through the air. There is an awesome moment when the aerialist must release the hands to which he or she has been holding, turn in the air, and grasp other hands waiting. What an act of faith that is! What a dangling moment in the changing! Many will see in it the parable of turning times in life when one must let go of old securities and grasp the new ones. To give assurance at such times may be part of pastoral care.

CONTEMPORARY CHANGES

Though the life progression is timeless, each generation reflects its own characteristics. This seems extraordinarily true of ours. Scientific and cultural changes are significant.

1. *Longevity.* One of these changes, of course, is the sheer fact of longer life. Paradoxically, to this point, this trend has been accompanied often by earlier retirement. As a result, many people find they have as much time in retirement as they had going to school

in the growing years. This can be a privilege or it can be a burden. While we already have seen major changes in the life-style of seniors, there certainly are more to come! The longer period of seniority for more people is a major factor in contemporary life, affecting marriages, medical care, family relationships, even political power. It also offers opportunity for enrichment—or embitterment. No human condition will face the church more persistently in these next years.

2. *Lengthened adolescence.* In a similar way, the uncommitted period of life which we have associated with adolescence has lengthened. Life-styles—to use the current term—have proliferated. One is the growing practice of young people living together without marriage. To most of them this is not an immorality, but a counter morality. It is too early to see what effect this is going to have on our continuing mores, but the probability of an enduring effect is very great. Are we moving into a time when between courtship and marriage there may be, for those who choose, an intermediate commitment? It is not easy for the church to face such questions. But they are here as young adulthood undergoes real cultural changes.

3. *New selfhood for women.* In a time of emerging liberations, women are effecting major changes in their place in our society. Impressive gains have been made in their right to choose their own places in our common life, freed from sexual discrimination. This inevitably brings adjustments in many other relationships: in the home and the rearing of children, in the choice of vocation, and in the way in which the years after child bearing will be spent. This right to selfhood for women is long overdue. Like any movement whose time has come, it may emerge at times in excessive or bizarre forms. But its main thrust is a part of the freedom which we believe God has commanded and promised in Christ.

If we had any doubt that life is closely interrelated, we have only to see how almost every aspect of our culture is affected by the changing status of women, including the way we live out some stages of the life cycle.

4. *Mobility.* In the church where I served as student minister, there was a memorable occasion marking a fiftieth wedding anniversary. But it was more than the usual occasion. Fifty years before, four couples had married in the same month. All of them had lived in that same village for the half century, and they celebrated their golden anniversaries together.

To be sure, that was extraordinary even then. But that same

community today is marked by mobility, by a population where there is constant coming and going. The so-called extended family does not remain without deliberate effort in our culture. Probably the grandparents are off somewhere with their trailer!

FINDING HELP IN OUR FAITH

If, as we have seen, unfolding life changes are both inescapable and irreversible, what support does the Christian faith give us? Where does it meet us at the crossings? Practical pastoral experience reveals two major contributions to seeing life through. These are essential contributions of faith to personal fulfillment.

A Sustaining Meaning

The Christian faith addresses our need for a *sustaining meaning in life.* Sometimes the contribution may even have to be stated less specifically: Christian faith assures us that there *is* a meaning, even when it seems obscure at any given time. We are supported by the faith that these changing experiences are not "sound and fury signifying nothing" but

> There is who heeds, who holds them all,
> In His large love and boundless thought.
>
> These struggling tides of life that seem
> In wayward, aimless course to tend,
> Are eddies of the mighty stream
> That rolls to its appointed end.[1]

Years ago our family was on a vacation trip in an area of the country we never had visited. In early evening we were driving through wide open spaces enjoying the new scenes and feeling comfortable in our relations with one another. During our conversation someone asked, "Are you sure this is the right road?" "Of course," I said easily. But the question found its mark. *Was* it the right road? As the question grew in our minds, something happened to us all. We grew silent; we leaned forward to peer out the window for the first road sign. A kind of tenseness appeared in all of us. Now it would be impressive to have a dramatic ending to the incident! But we just stopped at a service station and asked! Then, confirmed that we were on the right road, something again happened to us. We relaxed; conversation began again; and in due time we were singing on our way. It was the same car, the same road, the same people. One thing was different. Meaning had been lost, then regained. There have been many occasions to remember this as a parable of the need for meaning in everyday life, especially the times when changes come and we must enter into new areas of our lives.

This note of life's meaning will find its way into pastoral preaching. Within the community of faith we can help one another renew that sustaining faith, the belief that God's loving intent is in the experiences of life. There will be many times when the pastor will preach on words like those spoken to Abraham, "Go from your country and your kindred and from your father's house to the land that I will show you" (Genesis 12:1). The *fact* of life is in the first part. All of us are under command to "go from your country and your kindred and from your father's house." But the *faith* is in the latter part, "into a land that I will show you." To impart that shared faith as simply as possible is an important part of the pastor's function.

Affirmation of the New

The Christian faith *helps us say yes to each new stage of life.* We already have noted that Erikson's progression is stated in terms of successive conflicts, from trust versus mistrust even in infancy to integrity versus despair in old age. Translated into theological terms it is as though God is saying at each stage of life, "See, I have set before you this day life and good, death and evil. . . . therefore choose life" (Deuteronomy 30:15, 19). Every study of the unfolding of life confirms that this decision confronts us at every stage. We say yes or no to life again and again; we *choose* life or death in the form of affirmation or denial. Choose—that's a word of profound importance in matters of faith. Faith gives us the courage to say yes.

Stated most simply then, the pastor participates in the process of life: affirmation and reaffirmation of ongoing life, and rejection of the negations which deny life. One often is surprised to learn from personal acquaintance or the reading of biography how the most fulfilled and seemingly triumphant lives have gone through this very process, deliberately saying yes to new conditions which come, often in the face of strong urges to retreat or drop out. Every stage of the life cycle requires our acceptance of its conditions, and faith is the way by which we "choose life."

THE PASTORAL ROLE

It is probable that the largest portion of the pastoral care within the congregation will be related to this area of life's transitions.

To carry through this ministry, the pastor will be involved in several ways.

Interpretation

There is the need for *interpretation*. Often the pastor can give context to the particular experience through which another is passing. It may be a word to help in self-understanding, giving one whose transition time has come some shared insight into what is happening. It may be a word to others affected by that transition, especially the family or those closest to the one changing.

Several stages of life most commonly require that interpretation. One of these is the time of *teenage separation*, the standing off from parents, often in some form of rebellion. This is a baffling and often hurtful time for both the teenager and the family. Within the context of the community of faith, understanding can be shared, helping those involved gain insight that such transition is a move toward life, difficult and awkward but necessary for personhood. While most of us have known this in theory, we are surprised by the pain in it when it comes. Then we all need reassurance that the process of separation is a command of life, no matter how traumatic it seems at the time.

Alan Paton, known to us best for his *Cry, Beloved Country,* has written in a moving fashion about the time of his son's adolescence:

> I see my son is wearing long trousers, I tremble at this;
> I see he goes forward confidently, he does not know so
>   fully his own gentleness.
> Go forward, eager and reverent child, see here I begin
>   to take my hands away from you,
> I shall see you walk careless on the edges of the precipice,
>   but if you wish you shall hear no word
>   come out of me;
> My whole soul will be sick with apprehension, but I
>   shall not disobey you.
> Life sees you coming, she sees you come with assurance
>   towards her,
> She lies in wait for you, she cannot but hurt you;
> Go forward, go forward, I hold the bandages and oint-
>   ments ready.[2]

Another time for interpretation is related to *aging*. Here one sees changes that often affect not only the one aging but also those who are close. The years when the parent becomes the dependent are difficult for all, bringing a major shift in concept. To recognize that these changes are real and at the same time to maintain the dignity of a loved one, even when senility sets in, often require counsel and repeated interpretation. A pastor who sees many go through such a time can be of genuine help. Often there are deep feelings to be dealt with in a family undergoing the changes which aging brings. For some there are feelings of guilt—guilt even about the resentment one may feel in being progressively tied down. Or it may be guilt, even grief, at having to put an aging parent into a nursing home. At this time the pastor's quiet and confidential counsel can help the whole family. Increasingly, the physician simply does not have time—nor sometimes the skills—to deal with the feelings which emerge as aging comes to a loved one.

Another time when interpretation is increasingly needful is during the *middle years of life* when the stresses seem to accumulate. Many pastors report that this is emerging as the largest single category of counseling. The middle years can be the most stressful in the whole life cycle. One psychiatrist friend says that people in their forties are the largest single group in his practice. He adds that most of them find their way through to more serene and liberated years later in life. The feelings to be dealt with may be the negative ones of resentment, anxiety, or depression.

The stresses of that time of life are many: Often one faces the teenage rebellion. There is the awareness that the upward movement in one's work may be coming to an end. It's a time when a marriage may need to find freshness and new intimacy. With it there often is added responsibility for one's aging parents. Underlying all these stresses comes, of course, even if not admitted, awareness that physical powers have peaked and show decline. To be with the middle-aged person to give support and understanding when these distresses are being encountered is a ministry which a pastor can neither neglect nor discount.

Celebration

An obvious, distinctive function is *sharing the ceremonies which mark the progressive stages of life.* In some churches these are sacraments. In all churches there are ceremonies of passage deep within the tradition.

For the pastor these times offer a unique opportunity to be related to people's lives. There is a special bond which grows among those who have shared in one of the ceremonies which mark human experience. The ceremony alone can be a passing occasion. But where there is a genuine personal caring, that ceremony can establish a relationship which is enduring and enriching.

Ceremony is a way of saying what we cannot put into words. Most of us cannot fully articulate the deepest feelings we have. Ceremony gives us an alternative symbolic way of saying it. No matter how much we love a child, for example, and want for him or her the fullest possible life, we only rarely can put that into words. But the service of baptism in a few moments puts into simple and moving drama what we feel about that child. Here is the affirmation of special worth and the conviction that he or she is precious in God's eyes. Here is the sense of belonging to the family of faith and the promise of Christian nurture. No words of ours can encompass all that. But the ceremony, where much is unspoken but deeply felt, can bring it all together in moving expression.

While tradition gives us a number of very old ceremonies which mark the times of life, it is my belief that there can be others. Ceremony is one way we express the conviction that the common traditions of life have religious significance. The "signs of God's address" are in these seemingly ordinary occasions.

Among such occasions are graduations, when the church may well include a brief service acknowledging the young people graduating, but, more than that, assuring them of the support of their family of faith. In the midst of the usual festivities of birthday observances, a few moments can be devoted to a brief ceremony thanking God for the gifts of life. Perhaps we can note retirements in a similar way, looking ahead to the years of greater leisure and service. The occasion of a family going from the congregation to take up residency somewhere else can be made an affirmation of the "ties that bind" and of God, in whom there is no separation.

It is a growing practice to include in the service of worship on a Sunday morning the concerns and celebrations of the congregation. Here are noted not only illnesses or bereavement but also causes for thanksgiving. This practice is not only the sign of a caring community, but it also expresses the Christian concept of God who meets us at the crossings of life.

THE PASTORING CHURCH

Pastoral care needs to be reflected more adequately in our church organization. We can order our congregational life in a way which reflects who and what we are as a church. In a very real way, the church is the pastor. While the title of office is carried by a particular person, the faith, the love, and the caring of the whole church are conveyed by the person with the title.

It is the pastor's responsibility to organize the life of the congregation so that "ministration" is in administration. The church of the immediate future may make major changes in the way it orders its life, seeking an order that reflects more faithfully its pastoral care.

One way is to recover the original meaning of "deacon" as "one who serves." The word can be made less official and more pastoral. There are many laymen and laywomen who have natural gifts which can be developed into the practice of the pastoral arts. Time should be given in the meetings of a diaconate or comparable board to deal with the ministry to persons. This service will add dignity and interest to the office and be a vast relief for those who have been asked to deal with trivia at many board meetings.

The pastor can make deacons partners in the gospel, carrying comfort and hope to people in the congregation. Some churches have found it useful to divide the parish, giving each deacon a pastoral responsibility for a section of the congregation. Others have found that increased awareness of the pastoral meaning of "deacon" is sufficient. But congregational life can be ordered with pastoral needs given priority.

GOD IN THE MIDST OF LIFE

One comes to the close of this chapter with a great sense of being related to human life at its deepest levels. From the pastorate one sees the whole drama of human life. Almost every human experience sooner or later is seen. While some, like the novelist, are content to describe that human scene, the pastor is an *involved* observer.

One conviction, born of seeing life in all its stages, is expressed in one person's observation, "There are no common people except those who make themselves common." Most persons' lives are full of disappointments and almost unending anxiety. Sometimes people seem to be petty and given to self-seeking. But over and above all these, average people, sometimes bearing incredible loads and facing things that cannot be changed, still take up their problems and walk with them with faith and courage.

The other conviction born out of living with people as their pastor is the unshakable conviction that every human life has meaning, not a meaning immediately apparent, and in some cases never apparent, but a meaning.

The one thing the observation of human lives will not sustain is that there is a *trivial* meaning. Human suffering is too great. One is brought to the conviction that living is either a greater tragedy than we had supposed or that it has a meaning far more profound than we could have dreamed. Human suffering will allow no shallow meaning. After a lifetime of ministry, I am persuaded that there is a meaning of immense dignity and that it is shown to us in Jesus Christ.

Most of all, the life cycle in all its infinite variations gives us a confirmation of the Christian belief that God is not far off but comes to us in the common experiences of life. This is one meaning of the incarnation. If we had to come to know and trust God only by intellectual processes, few of us would qualify, for by ability and training we would falter. If it required some special aesthetic ability so that we could "see God," there would be only an elite, for, as Browning said, "God has a few of us whom he whispers in the ear." But the Christian faith is that God addresses us in the common experiences of life; he meets us at the crossings we all must cross. He is found in the mainstream of living, in the experiences we all have.

That at some time to some degree to some people we may be present in the experiences of transition and help them see that God is there is the immense privilege of ministry in the life cycle.

Chapter 7

The Pastor
and Social Concern

In his play, *The Hostage,* Brendan Behan has a scene in which an old man is recounting for a small group of intrigued listeners the part he had in the Irish Rebellion. As he tells the story, he relives it, until at the end he is completely caught up. At the peak of his excitement he suddenly turns to a young girl standing in the group and confronts her, "Why are you getting so upset over Ireland?—Where . . . were you in nineteen-sixteen when the real fighting was going on?" Completely taken back, she manages to stammer, "I wasn't born." At this the old man turns to the others and with the air of one bearing a great tribulation says, "You're full of excuses!"[1]

Many times in our twentieth century we have lived in that kind of intensity. Such strong feeling is only one of many evidences that this indeed is an era of far-reaching social upheaval. Professor Pitirim Sorokin has expressed the judgment that only four times in the whole human story have we had a crisis as fundamental and far-reaching as ours.[2]

In such a crucial situation, it is appropriate that the pastor bring a dimension of social concern to the ministry. Our theological seminaries have brought the study of Christian justice and social change into the curriculum. Our major denominations deal with

77

public issues at their stated gatherings, and many have had departments giving full time to the Christian impact on social issues. As a result, many contemporary pastors enter the parish ministry with a commitment to social involvement, the redemption of a society deeply in trouble. Indeed, they count this as part of their call.

IN RESPONSE TO OUR TIME

The social concern often found in the contemporary pastor has deep historic roots. For well over a century that concern has been emerging; it has been tested and refined and confronted by challenge after challenge in the events and movements which mark the modern world.

Perhaps the protest against slavery was an important beginning. At its end, it brought Edward Beecher to say, "Now that God has smitten slavery unto death, he has opened the way for the redemption and sanctification of our whole social system."[3] Upon that belief a growing body of able men and women sought to arouse the churches to "the application of the teachings of Jesus and the total message of the Christian salvation to society, to the economic life, and the social institutions as well as to individuals," as one of its leaders, Shailer Mathews, put it.[4]

In the rather sanguine belief that this indeed was to come about, a magazine reorganized in 1900 took the title *The Christian Century*. Many hoped and believed the twentieth century would be described by that title.

Yet who could have foreseen what that century would bring forth? From 1914 on it has been the story of world wars, of the rise of great secular religions such as Communism, of revolution and upheaval (three-fourths of the world's people have undergone revolution in our century, one-half since World War II). More recently it has brought racial confrontation and widespread alienation of youth.

At the same time, amazing potential has appeared. We have seen emerging world communities, the rise of many new nations in Africa and Asia following the death of colonialism. So the contemporary Christian faces a contradiction. It seems that God again confronts us with the biblical word. "See, I have set before you this day life and good, death and evil . . . therefore choose life." Because the Christian word intersects this recent history, the pastor goes into his or her parish ministry today in the hope of sharing the social imperatives of this generation. By so doing, a person makes a deep and genuine

Christian response to the challenge of God's word in our time.

AN HONEST, SOMETIMES TROUBLED APPRAISAL

Such a commitment often brings a series of questions: Does social concern fit into parish ministry? What if the congregation does not share the pastor's commitment to social change? Where does work for justice fit into the whole of the pastor's responsibility? One must come to terms with such basic questions.

1. *There is the honest question: Does it do any good?* Doesn't realism require us to face the hard truth that social struggles center around power structures, and the church with its ways of persuasion usually is quite ineffective in such an arena?

Edwin Dahlberg whose ministry has borne a lifetime witness to social concern has a story to illustrate how some people feel about the church's attempt to be involved in social issues. A friend said to Dr. Dahlberg that the church trying to deal with social issues reminded him of a bantam rooster let loose in a barnyard filled with large-hoofed dray horses. The rooster spent his time dodging the hooves and saying, "Now, brethren, let us be careful not to trample on one another!" Well, are our efforts no more effective?

The question of effectiveness is disturbing. When one sees all that has come to pass in the twentieth century, it is a wonder that we even talk about the possibility of change at all. In the very time when more people have worked for peace, we have had more wars and of a scope never imagined. Albert Camus's reluctant conclusion that we live under a "benign indifference" came in part from the fact that seventy-five million people had died or been made homeless by war in his brief lifetime. Right in the middle of our century we learned of the Holocaust when over six million Jews were put to death in unprecedented genocide. In many ways racism which sets race against race is more widespread, though in a different form. Why, then, don't we accept the seemingly inescapable conclusion that there's not much we can do for a better world?

To ask this question is to come upon the astounding theological context for social action. By that view, the question whether it does any good is irrelevant. This is another case where the "foolishness of God is wiser than men." Christian social action can offer no guarantees that it will achieve its goal. Sometimes the odds seem strongly against it. Yet we are not without hope. Why? There are two reasons.

First, the main question is not, what is expedient, but what is obedient? When Jesus revealed that God's mission is to "set at liberty those who are bruised," it left us no alternative. As Phillips Brooks said, "There is a necessary limit to our achievement but none to our attempt. . . . We must answer for our actions; God will answer for our powers." That conviction gives a peculiar staying power to Christian social concern. This does mean, of course, that we are to bring very careful discernment to the strategy of social justice. The commission to be involved is clear.

Second, however it may be stated, there is an eschatological hope. This is not an esoteric doctrine of history. It is the truth that at the last, at a time he will choose, and in a way pleasing to him, God's will *does* prevail. We sometimes have forgotten this truth and fallen into an unfolding "success story" view of the social struggle. In short, we took the cross out of our struggle. But we took the resurrection out of our hopes, too. In the gospel story we see the basis for the Christian hope. To be sure, to follow that course sometimes seems to ask too much of us in faithfulness. But the story carries a motivation and a hope which have put endurance in the souls of men and women.

2. *A second question faced by pastors is whether social concern can really fit into the pastoral setting.* Can one be both pastor and prophet? Doesn't the pastor have to stand close to people, and the prophet on occasion stand off against them? How then can one do both?

The answer to that is not theoretical, but practical, or more exactly, biographical. There is an impressive list of those who HAVE done both. From the witness of their ministries we can see that instead of working against each other, the prophetic and the pastoral really support each other. Caring is still caring, whether it is for those who are in the close, personal fellowship of a church, or for those who are outcasts and disadvantaged.

One thinks of a minister like Ernest Fremont Tittle, a longtime pastor of the First Methodist Church in Evanston, Illinois. For thirty years his social passion was imparted from the pulpit, especially in the area of world peace. When war came and a hostile press was determined to silence his voice, the church stood loyally by though many did not agree with him. One layman put it directly, "I may not agree with Ernest Tittle on his social views. But when my wife died, he walked along the lake with me for most of the night. And when a man who cares that much speaks, I for one intend to listen."

To be sure, it is part of pastoral responsibility to find the level of tolerance a congregation has for the stress of controversial subjects. It is the further responsibility, in my judgment, to help persons develop more mature levels. That growth seems to come by using the freedom we have.

In fact, on occasion the pastor will need to interpret the meaning of that freedom in a congregation. For there are *two* freedoms in any church. One, of course, is the freedom of the *pulpit*. While held to being responsible, a pastor cannot be told what he must preach or what he may not. In fact, it often seems that most preachers have far more freedom than they use. But the second freedom is that of the *pew*. No one can tell those who worship that they must come or that they may not; that they must accept a given position or that they may not. Both freedoms are essential to congregational life. We believe that between these two freedoms there is room for new and better understanding than that held by either pulpit or pew. To interpret this heritage until it becomes part of the common understanding of a congregation is one teaching function of the pastor.

HANDLING SOCIAL CONCERN RESPONSIBLY

We need to be as practical as possible in this matter. The very union of the pastoral and the prophetic, of which we have been speaking, requires us to use every skill we have in ministry. Able contemporary pastors who have accepted involvement in social issues, yet were faithful pastors to their people, give us good witness. From their experience several practical points can be helpful, six in all.

1. *The pastor will be far more educator than agitator.* This is not to imply that strong positions do not need to be taken. At times, even at the risk of confrontation, they do! But pastoral relations require the longer view. As in political life, one often has to begin by "practicing the possible." It should be added that the "possible" often is much more than most assume and many fear. And there are times when one must go beyond what seems immediately possible because anything else would be a loss of integrity.

What is at stake here is whether the *church itself* can be awakened to new issues of justice and compassion. A church has not done its part when it tolerates the *minister's* taking a forward position on social issues. The real hope is to bring the congregation to new understanding of what is happening in our time and of the place of the committed Christian community in the world. An awakened and aroused church is the most far-reaching and ongoing result of a socially concerned ministry. Not only does a congregation see the fuller implications of the gospel, but also a committed church insures a more enduring witness for social righteousness.

2. *The socially concerned pastor will learn to listen as well as speak!* When differences arise, few people, except those who have some neurotic need, will insist that everyone agree with them. But almost everyone will insist that they be *heard*—and rightly so. To be sure, for some, the only evidence that will convince them they have been heard is agreement with them! But it is immensely helpful, and often adequate, for the pastor to give evidence that he or she is genuine and painstaking in the desire to hear opposing or alternate views. Everyone gains by that. The pastor really learns a great deal and often finds the need to change or modify his or her views. But even if that does not happen, the other person feels *respected* and, therefore, feels no need to go on the defensive.

In short, many tensions which seem to be over issues are really evidence of a basically poor human relationship. It often means that someone is feeling put down and unaccepted. To be understood is one form of acceptance, even when it does not lead to agreement. To seek such understanding is part of the pastoral approach to persons.

3. *The pastor will need to come to terms with his or her own feelings.* Any kind of stress, whether over a personal difference or a social issue, brings to the surface many submerged feelings! These often catch us by surprise. When stress comes, we learn a great deal not only about the issues involved but also about ourselves! We sense how much hostility or defensiveness or demand for dominance there is in us. The different views can become a contest of egos! Churches are especially susceptible to that malady.

It is hoped that the years in theological education will provide opportunities to gain insight into one's own emotional needs. Many schools do provide such opportunities through small group experience, personal counseling, or clinical training. Here one gains insight into his or her own needs. We talk about sin in the classroom. We encounter it in the small group. Here we come to terms with our hostilities, our excessive dependence, our need to dominate or to put others down, our inability to stand opposition, and our longing to be ministered unto rather than to minister. If these are unresolved, a time of differences over social issues may bring them out—with a vengeance! No one needs greater emotional maturity than a prophet under fire.

This matter of the emotional maturity of the minister, of course, touches the whole of pastoral practice. This is not to impose an impossible standard of perfection. We preach that all are sinners. Here is one place where we practice what we preach! A part of that maturity is the readiness to accept one's humanness, one's angers, insecurities, and fallibilities. Is not maturity the ability to be comfortable with what we are and what we are not? Then we can enter into differences of opinion without using them to resolve our own emotional needs.

This leads us to face a basic question about a pastor's relation to a congregation. We shouldn't "use" a congregation to feed our emotional needs or establish our self-esteem. To be sure, there *are* fulfillments and securities which come from being related to a congregation in a healthy way. But we have to have someplace else to stand. That place is in the very faith and experience proclaimed to others. It is in the gospel itself, the audacious trust that our reliance on God is the ground of our being. It means that the approval of a congregation, the sense of support and love, and the assurance of effectiveness are gifts of grace, over and above. In short, we gratefully accept these great gifts, "not because we must but because we may." This, it seems to me, is maturity in ministry, and it is especially put to the test when conflict comes.

4. Where social issues are involved, *the pastor will need to make every effort to get all the facts available.* In short, we must be sure to do our homework!

An able layman, himself deeply involved with social concerns, has observed that he does not object to his pastor dealing with such issues, but he does object to his doing it so poorly! Most of the decisions with which we are faced in the modern world are complex. Before we go on to advocacy, there must be credibility, the evidence that we have taken time to learn the extent of the problem, the ways which are being attempted to meet it, and the procedures by which changes have to come about. Sometimes we jump to conclusions when we ought to walk, observing as we go.

It would be absurd to suppose that we could be authorities on all the issues which affect human life! But that doesn't mean that we "turn it over to those who know" or make no attempt to inform ourselves. After all, even as citizens we assume the right—and the ability—to be informed. For the pastor who would be socially concerned this homework is essential.

As I review my ministry, I am amazed at the diversity—and urgency—of the issues where human values were at stake.

As I began, there were the problems attendant upon a depression. Unemployment was real, and the nation was undergoing rapid and widespread economic changes.

Then came World War II and the decisions related to that tragic time: our involvement, conscientious objection, the feeding of peoples. Universal military conscription was making its bid. There was the planning for the peace.

There followed the McCarthy era when civil rights was the issue and the rights of free speech and dissent were threatened.

Particularly urgent were the racial decisions from integration to confrontation. There was also the matter of rights of other minorities, particularly the rights of women. Equally, many were troubled by the alienation of youth and the impact of the counter moralities.

All of these issues touch the Christian concern, for they deal with the well-being of people and as such are part of the mission of the church. Deep within them is the issue of justice and social righteousness.

We are indebted to denominational and ecumenical departments which have sought to give our churches basic facts and materials. Also, particular lay persons in the church often are resources to be sought. Often study groups can be formed around particular issues. These are ways we avoid generalities which have little effect upon real decisions and in fact may divert from them.

5. *The pastor needs to clarify and respect the essential role religious faith has in social justice.* Pastors sometimes feel at least one step removed from the practical social issues. And they often are, but not always. There are occasions when the church mobilizes and speaks with an impressive voice. That voice probably was determinative, for example, in passing the Civil Rights Bill. We know that those in political power do follow the pronouncements of the churches on current issues. In a biography of Eleanor Roosevelt it was noted that President Roosevelt knew that the time had come for bold action on racial matters when the women of the Methodist Church in the South adopted a statement to that effect.

But even when the church does not take specific action, it is doing something essential for social righteousness. It is dealing with belief—the most powerful force on earth. That belief has aroused the conscience of men and women in the face of wrongs. Today it supports those who are engaged in their own liberation and quickens the sense of justice to which they can appeal. That belief gives us the energy to see through the fight against the madness of war in a generation which already has massive overkill. As long as the church keeps alive the belief in human dignity and the demands of the neighbor, it IS doing something—something without which the passion and energy for social justice would fail.

At the same time the church contributes to another priceless ingredient for social change—*integrity*. Even the best intentioned have the problems of compromise in the midst of the ambiguities of social struggle. But without personal integrity at the center we run off into cynical self-seeking. Bonhoeffer says it for us:

> *Are we still of any use?* . . . What we shall need is not geniuses, or cynics, or misanthropes, or clever tacticians, but plain, honest, straightforward men. Will our inward power of resistance be strong enough, and our honesty with ourselves remorseless enough, for us to find our way back to simplicity and straightforwardness?[5]

So one looks at the stern realities of social conflict: the stubborn self-interest which guides our actions, the rationalization that justifies our position of privilege, the grabs for power which mark every human enterprise, the proximate nature of all gains, and the sinfulness of people which enables them to do things in social groups they wouldn't think of doing personally. In the face of these has the church any contribution? The biblical insistence upon human dignity and integrity stands off against these things. We CAN make a difference. And in that difference, the pastor as such has a distinctive contribution.

The present hour has revealed that perhaps the greatest contribution of all is a *sturdy hope which is theologically grounded.* Generation after generation, the Christian community of faith has spoken expectantly of the kingdom of God. The kingdom never has been something which persons alone would "build." It can be served by faithful men and women now, but its consummation is in God's hands, in the time and way which he chooses. This hope, so easily pushed aside by moderns as "unrealistic," strangely endures while other human hopes have receded in our time. And that hope makes all the difference in the world now, for a world with hope is alive and a world without hope already is dying.

Professor Werner Lemke was a boy in Germany during World War II. As the war was drawing to a close, the Allied forces came at last to his home and the family had to move out. He relates that he has a vivid memory of gathering a few things for hurried flight. They had a sense of ending and impending defeat. At the last moment, however, when they stopped for a final look at the home in which they had grown up, an older brother said, "Wait a minute." He went back to the piano where they had gathered so often as a family and played one verse of the hymn "O God, our help in ages past, Our hope for years to come!"

That's the kind of hope we serve. It is grounded not in the nature of the human situation at a given time, but in the nature of God. He will not be put to ultimate defeat. That assurance may prove in its sturdy audacity to be the most practical contribution of the biblical faith to our social hopes. As long as the church proclaims that hope by word and manner of life, it need not question its relevance to the human hope for a better world.

Chapter 8

The Pastoral Role in Public Worship

Through the years, there have been many occasions to recall the remarks of a little girl who once worshiped in our church. She was being brought up Roman Catholic but on this Sunday morning attended our Baptist service with her grandmother, a member of the church. As she left, the child remarked, as reported by her family, "Grandmother, I think I like your service better. You make it up as you go along."

Even we who are at home in nonliturgical churches wonder at times whether she was not right! In a secular day which has lost the transcendent sense of life and seems to get along quite well without it, most pastors have to engage in the leadership of public worship, a role for which we often have received little preparation. We who do not have prescribed liturgies of worship have to show a creativeness on our own which is more than "making it up as we go along." Nothing is more important than meaningful corporate worship.

What then is the concept of worship in the free church? What part does a pastor have in it?

QUALITIES OF FREE CHURCH WORSHIP

While the so-called free churches generally have not placed

major emphasis on liturgy, they, in fact, have brought some special qualities to public worship. These are important to pastoral practice. Many of us have our heritage and our home in churches which are basically autonomous, which have a strong evangelical tone in the preaching, and rest upon a confessional but noncreedal basis. Inevitably, churches of this kind reflect something of their essential character in their worship, and that character has qualities important to pastoral concern.

Willard L. Sperry once wrote:

> So long as the church bids men to the worship of God and provides a simple and credible vehicle for worship it need not question its place, mission, and influence in the world. If it loses faith in the act of worship, is thoughtless in the ordering of worship, and careless in the conduct of worship, it need not look to its avocations to save it. It is dead at its heart, and no chafing of the extremities, producing what Carlyle called "quaint galvanic sprawlings" will bring back the life that has left it.[1]

But in what ways is worship essential to pastoral practice?

Person-Mindedness

For one thing, such public worship has been marked by discernible *person-mindedness.* Worship in nonliturgical churches has not submerged the personality of the minister by making him or her subject to prescribed forms which allow no individuality. The preacher is known as a person addressing other persons. He or she does not merely speak for the faith of the church in general. The minister's word is expected to carry a note of personal witness. Thus the very situation which often we decry, namely, that the church is built around a person instead of around the Christian faith, is a corruption of a basically important quality—the respect for individuality and the personal aspects of the encounter in worship.

On the other side of the encounter is the deeply personal nature of the response. The message itself is not a proclamation in general but in particular. It often has the quality of a letter written and personally addressed rather than a word posted "to whom it may concern." This personal aspect of worship in the free churches is not without its corruptions. It can move into an intense individualism which thrusts itself into the center and displaces any concept of a whole people of God. But it would be a profound loss if in our search for more order in worship and by our use of historic liturgies we should lose that personal quality. One writer could say of Wesley, Whitefield, and Spurgeon that, while other men forgot the individual in the crowd, these men forgot the crowd in remembering the individual. It is a distinction to be cherished.

Centrality of the Bible and Preaching

Beside this is the consistent *centrality of the Bible and preaching.* To lose sight of that truth in any service of worship would result in an incomparable loss. Granted that much of our preaching falls far short of being "the most important thing that ever happens upon this earth," the need is not the substitution of something else but a recovery of preaching in its more dynamic form.

As a matter of fact, preaching and liturgy cannot be set against each other, for they both rest upon the same foundation of faith. They are both branches of the same vine. Without a basic belief in the self-disclosure of God in Jesus Christ, neither preaching nor liturgy has any real ground upon which to stand. We obviously cannot expect the word of God to come to us in preaching if we do not believe in a self-disclosing God. The loss of dynamic in preaching is the result of the same emptiness which causes the loss of dynamic in worship. In either case it rests upon a basic belief in God's self-disclosure in Jesus Christ. Whether the minister stands in the pulpit or at the Communion table, the only ground for doing so is the basic belief that this is more than human action. It is God acting through these means. Almost inevitably, therefore, if we lose confidence in preaching, we also must surrender our expectation in liturgy; for there is no evidence that God has withdrawn his action from one and transferred it to the other. In this sense, the service of worship must be seen as a whole. It is a total act of confidence in God's self-revelation.

It may be helpful to recall in this regard that the same dialogue which marks the biblical record is also the dialogue seen in a service of worship. It has been noted that the biblical word is addressed in at least three directions: some of it is human word addressed to God; some of it is God's word addressed to people; and some of it is the word of person to person about God. These same three aspects of the word must be found in the service of worship. We have placed special emphasis upon the word of God to people, and that word has come through preaching. This is an insight not to be lost in the midst of our interest in liturgical revival.

Congregational Fellowship

Consider another value to be cherished. It is the *dimension of congregational fellowship* which is so evident in our services. To be sure, this quality also has its corruptions and its counterfeits. We are all aware of churches which have substituted a false cordiality for a real acceptance. The mood of the service can become "the more we get together, the happier we will be." But real worship must preserve that dimension which relates us to one another. The biblical word says again and again that God has spoken to us as Joseph spoke to his brothers, "You shall not see my face unless your brother be with you."

In King's Chapel, Boston, the worshiper may enter the church and be ushered into a pew which is so constructed that no one around can be seen because of the high partitions. The pulpit is elevated so that the worshiper and others in the pew can lift up their eyes and see the preacher who is bringing the word, but they cannot see the other worshipers in their pews. While one certainly can understand the concept of the builders who wanted to keep all diversions and distractions from those who were being confronted by the word of God, it is an approach essentially without biblical support. For there is a triangle of relationship even in worship, and the obedience God requires of us must issue out in our new relations with one another. Rauschenbusch put this into a word of personal witness: "When I'm in the consciousness of God, my fellow men are not far off and forgotten, but close and strangely dear."[2] To be sure, in our free churches our emphasis upon fellowship has been so marked that we often lose the God-consciousness in the excessive neighbor-consciousness. But it is a dimension to be corrected, not to be lost.

Flexibility

There is yet another quality to be noted in our free worship. It is *flexibility.* There is a strength in knowing that changing forms may still proclaim unchanging reality. Jesus Christ *is* the same yesterday, today, and forever, but we are not. He addresses us at the point of our deepest needs, and those needs change. While forms of worship necessarily are revised slowly, we must reserve the right to keep them real and contemporary.

In this regard the flexibility in forms of worship is not unlike the unending enterprise of translating the Scriptures. As the changes which come in the new translations are designed to keep the original word intact and understandable, so the changes in forms of worship must be to the end of keeping the Good News fresh and accessible. Speaking of translation, the preface to the King James Version of the

Bible in 1611 included the simple and poetic declaration, "Translation it is that openeth the window, to let in the light; that breaketh the shell, that we may eat the kernel; that putteth aside the curtain, that we may look into the most holy places; that removeth the cover of the well, that we may come by the water." It is a strength to be cherished that free church worship can "translate" the Living Word into contemporary forms of worship which faithfully express to a given time the timeless Good News.

It may be said that the living water of the gospel flows through many kinds of terrain. As a stream takes on the form of the terrain through which it is flowing, sometimes moving through broad fields and at other times rushing and tumbling through rocky rapids, so the gospel word may be proclaimed in changing categories. Like the other values we have mentioned, there is a danger here. Out of control, this adaptability can lead into the bizarre or the superficial. But the dangers of rigidity are greater and the flexibility of free worship is a distinction to be kept.

To speak of these values is to be reminded that all have been hard won throughout our history. Many of them were born as protest against other religious systems and practices which seemed to have become authoritarian, violating the freedom of soul which must be respected in every person.

THE EXTENDED EVENT OF JESUS CHRIST

Now we must ask: What is the underlying theme which gives Christian worship its unity and coherence? Is worship primarily a promotional gathering, a form of ecclesiastical sales meeting by which our enthusiasm to be about the business of the Lord is restored? Is it a "search for God," the lifting up of our deepest aspirations? Or is it a time for instruction in "moral and spiritual values"? In practice, all of these to some degree at some time have been common forms of worship.

But for the Christian there is a more audacious meaning, a tremendous leap of faith—the affirmation that Christian worship must be understood as a *continuation of the event of Jesus Christ in human life.* It is, as P. T. Forsyth put it, the way by which the gospel "proclaims and prolongs itself."[3]

The heart of worship, then, is in the New Testament word, used regularly at the Lord's Supper, but equally applicable whenever we gather for worship, "This do in remembrance of me." In worship we are discovering once again what never should be forgotten: God's great act in Jesus Christ is open-ended. The old, old story is a continued story. What Churchill said at a crucial point in our history may be said of the earthly life of Jesus Christ, "This is not the beginning of the end, but the end of the beginning."

The biblical witness not only declares this truth, but also it shouts it. More exactly, it sings it! The New Testament is the witness of a people who made the tremendous discovery that the event of Jesus Christ was going on in spite of all that men could do. It was not difficult for them to believe in the resurrection. In the light of their experience it would have been difficult for them to believe anything else. The livingness of Jesus Christ was their most authentic experience. They laid hold on great promises and found them true. "For where two or three are gathered in my name, there am I in the midst of them" (Matthew 18:20). The New Testament words we cherish are only expressions of their experience. "Greater works than these will he do" (John 14:12). If it was true that "in Christ God was reconciling the world to himself," then the rest also must be so, "entrusting to us the message of reconciliation" (2 Corinthians 5:19). Then there was the final assurance, "Lo, I am with you always" (Matthew 28:20). Either we are embarked on the most audacious enterprise to which we can give ourselves or on our most tragic delusion.

When we firmly place this central truth at the heart of our worship, we have made the essential move toward reality and authenticity. We have established a criterion for determining the order which should prevail in a Christian service of worship. We have set the two notes which should be in the service: remembrance and expectancy. We have moved away from the purely subjective to the objective, from something we expect to do to ourselves to the expectancy that God in his way and in his own time will do his work in us. Talk about a leap of faith!

Let us keep in mind that remembrance of Jesus Christ does not mean "looking back." It means looking at the present in the light of that memory. Full worship is based upon the conviction about which we sing in the Gloria Patri, "As it was in the beginning, is now and ever shall be, world without end"—and the emphasis must be on the words "is now." Thus, we express the faith that where the word of Christ is heard, the work of Christ goes on. Thus is the event of Jesus Christ extended.

ORDERING THE EVENT

If this faith is the central meaning of Christian worship, then it suggests an order for the service. Perhaps our model is in the beautiful story of the walk to Emmaus (Luke 24:13-35). Consider how it unfolds. Two came together to start the journey, talking "with each other about all these things that had happened," but not understanding their significance. Then it was that Jesus, unrecognized, fell into step with them and interpreted the Scriptures. When they arrived, he went in to the table with them "and their eyes were opened and they recognized him." From that moment of recognition some great things happened. Their past experience was redeemed, "Did not our hearts burn within us while he talked to us on the road?" Actually there was no evidence that they felt that way at the time. It was experience *reclaimed* after the recognition. And from that, "they rose that same hour and returned to Jerusalem." The elements of a service of worship are on the Emmaus road: the interpretation of the Scripture, the hopes for moments of disclosure like that which took place at the table, and the return to the very place from which they had come, but this time with their hearts burning within them. Interpretation, recognition, and return!

John E. Skoglund has suggested a similar appropriate order for the service. The elements are: Preparation, Liturgy of the Word, Liturgy of the Table, Response, and Return.

The Preparation would include the opening biblical sentences which remind us of God's presence, the hymn of praise which is the response to that reminder, the confession or the invocation which reminds us of God's majesty and the promise of his forgiveness. Thus we make ourselves ready.

There follows the Liturgy of the Word which must include, of course, the Scriptures, a prayer or ascription offering ourselves for the receiving of God's Word, and then the sermon.

Here we come to the point at which our worship services are being challenged by this suggested order. For actually or symbolically we should sit down together at the Lord's Table. Some churches may choose to observe Communion with the elements present and distributed more frequently than the customary once a month. Even if not, the portion of the service which follows the sermon may gather the elements of fellowship which the table represents. Here we will pray for one another. Here we will bring our gifts. Here we will be mindful of the fellowship, the family of Christ. Here are the concerns and celebrations. As John E. Skoglund puts it: "This means that any liturgy which is complete must include both the reading and preaching of the Word and observance of the Lord's Supper.... Even if the communion is left out, it will be symbolically present in the offering and the prayers which bring the service to completion."[4]

The service will close with Response and Return. The final part of the service may be looked upon as a transition and not a termination, the going out following our coming in. Thus the event of Jesus Christ is further extended into our common life. When our worship is real, we are not only girded against the world but also commissioned to go into it.

THE PASTOR'S RESPONSIBILITY

We have taken more time to deal with the meaning of worship in general than might have been expected in a book which deals with pastoral practice. Yet this emphasis reflects a conviction that the most urgent need for many pastors is a recovery—or discovery—of meaning in that in which they are engaged every week. More often than we like to admit, our leadership of worship shows that we really have little concept of its unifying meaning. The pastor thereby lessens the effectiveness of this aspect of his or her ministry. So we have acknowledged that the understanding of what we are about is probably our most urgent need.

Particularly when we are considering ministry in a secular culture, it is obvious that to provide worship of high order is a ministry which resides almost exclusively in the church. We ought to do it well, and several leads are open to us:

1. *Worship is not one person leading and all others listening.* This mistaken concept requires some deliberate corrective steps in the average Protestant congregation. We have a great tradition, of course, in the congregational singing. Here one feels the whole community of faith praising God.

There can be other ways in which the congregation plays an active part. The Scripture can be read by a member of the church who comes up from the congregation. Even if there needs to be some practice during the week so that the reading can be heard, it is worth it for the symbol of a participating community which such reading provides.

With a little careful study there can be more congregational responses. Before the sermon, the minister can say, "Let the words of my mouth"; and the congregation can respond, "And the meditations of my heart"; then all can say, "Be acceptable in Thy sight, O Lord, my strength and my redeemer."

One even hopes the congregation will feel free to say "Amen" at points in the service which are particularly meaningful. The minister sensitive to these points may even take the lead in saying, "And all the people said," to which the congregation responds, "Amen." Even the pastoral prayer may be broken up into three prayers to which the people can say the "Amen." On occasions such as the Communion service the people may be encouraged to extend the peace of God to one another.

In short, there is a freshening of worship which comes from the concept of congregational celebration, in contrast to the congregation as "audience." We are discovering what should have been evident enough in the witness of the Psalms and devotional passages in the Bible, namely, the active participation of the congregation. Such participation is not a denial of the holy solemnity of worship, but a recognition that a component of that solemnity is joy.

It will fall to the pastor to introduce and strengthen this lay participation. Generally, lay men and women cannot invite themselves!

2. This suggests, in fact, that the *responsibility for educating the church in worship rests with the minister*. We need to interpret to congregations how the service is the continuation of the Christ event. To the board of deacons, or some other official board, has been delegated the responsibility for the services of worship. Time at a board meeting can be set aside for the discussion of worship and for the interpretation of the various elements.

On occasion that interpretation can come into sermons. Also, the newsletter can be a means of education, especially as new elements are introduced. Adult education classes ought to deal with the meaning of worship. All these together will have marked effect on the congregation, giving them the real fulfillment of understanding, perhaps for the first time, of what worship is about.

3. *The services of worship as well as the sermon have to have careful preparation each week*. There is an impressive body of material to assist the minister and we should be well acquainted with such books as John E. Skoglund's *A Manual of Worship*.[5]

We have falsely believed that preparation may stifle spontaneity. Some are afraid of anything that hints at "formalism." But there is no such thing as "formless" services. The question is: will it be good form, with language of dignity fitting worship, or poor form, with language which is repetitious or convoluted or a mere stringing together of phrases which have the sound of piety? Anything done as often as public worship takes on form! Listen to the prayers that are supposed to be spontaneous and discover how often we are spontaneous about the same things in the same way! It is sometimes hard to distinguish between inspiration and desperation. There is no reason inspiration cannot come on Saturday in the quiet of one's study instead of Sunday morning facing a congregation where the words come out because one has to say something rather than because one has something to say!

4. In the churches which put their emphasis upon the local congregation the pastor should take care to reflect in the service the *continuity of the Christian faith.* Many of us convey the impression that the whole enterprise began when our congregation was founded. We sometimes act as though nothing much of importance happened between the resurrection and the revival which gave birth to our congregation!

In worship a people's history becomes a personal one. This is an important part of our belonging. Whenever we gather the people of God in Christ's name, we are affirming that it was *we* who came out of Egypt; it was *we* who stood at Golgotha. But we need to go on and affirm that it was we who bore the early persecutions, endured the indignities, engaged in the intellectual encounters which defined the faith, and followed every frontier, planting in each new clearing the seeds of the historic faith. Our worship can and should sing,

> "For all the saints, who from their labors rest, . . .
> Thy name, O Jesus, be forever blest."

I was working in my yard one day when I tried to brush aside a twig. But it would not be brushed aside. When I tried to pick it up, more and more of it appeared. It turned out to be not a twig at all but the end of a root, and the root was attached to a tree. That thing had connections! It's a fitting discovery that no church is merely local, either in its history or its responsibilities or its relationships. To celebrate the meaning of our being a historic community is not the first business of worship, but it is a reminder of one of God's mighty acts in history—the appearance of his people.

5. One of the growing practices is for the *pastor to gather the*

concerns and celebrations of members and share them with the congregation.
We once assumed that this kind of personal reference was inconsistent with the ordered service of dignity. But we have discovered that such warm, personal concern does fit in with the service and, in fact, enriches it; for it is an expression of what we are as Christian congregations.

One thinks of the way in which the apostle Paul included personal references in his letters, usually at the close. Here, as at few places, one senses the nature of the first Christian congregation—the concern persons had for one another, their mutual support and sharing.

In similar way, the regular inclusion of concerns and celebrations, usually at the close of the service, has proved consistent with our nature. As Christ ministered to individuals, so such remembrance of persons seems to have a rightful place in a service which remembers him.

These personal items may be spoken from the congregation at the minister's invitation. Or they may be gathered by the minister, especially when she or he has made the deacons aware of the need to know about those who should be included. Many churches have started the practice on Communion Sunday, but some have included it in the regular Sunday worship, feeling it is a true expression of the event of Christ among us.

NO GREATER PRIVILEGE

The continuation of the event of Jesus Christ! Is that belief or make-believe? Can he walk among us still, making us whole, gathering the lonely into fellowship, calling the strong to serve him, helping us see God in our everyday life? Can the incarnation extend even into our secular day?

Pastors will learn that in the privilege of leading worship we establish ties with people who need our ministry as at no other time in the week. And when we see how the broken loaf of our efforts has been a means of grace to people, we will have good times when we will be "lost in wonder, love, and praise" at the sheer privilege of it.

Chapter 9

The
Personal Equation

Most of us readily recognize the truth in Santayana's observation, "Nothing requires a rarer intellectual heroism than willingness to see one's equation written out."[1] Yet, heroic or not, some evaluation of one's inner life is needed. No consideration of pastoral practice would be complete without some dealing with the personal life of the minister.

In our tolerant moods we sometimes admit that there are two sides to every question. What is not as readily seen is that often one is the outside and the other is the inside!

Every calling develops its private world. Each has its own language, its mores, its values, its criteria of judgment, its assumed adversaries, even its inside jokes. The ministry is no exception. What does that private life of the minister look like in the contemporary culture?

RELATIONSHIPS

We have noted several times in these pages that the minister by virtue of office is admitted to the primary experiences in the lives of people. By primary we mean those experiences which are basic, in common with all men and women, and which we associate with being human. Usually these are the relationships which form human life—parent and child, and love and hate relationships, the face-to-face relationships where our deepest emotions are involved. Birth, death, illness, crisis, and transition, on the one hand, and the great joys on the other, the hours of self-discovery and achievement, the times of recovery and triumph, the hidden moral victories.

In every person there is a core of personhood. Here the external distinctions between people fade away. At that center of being, one loves and is loved, seeks to come to terms with childhood images of one's self and one's world, harbors one's secret anxieties, and finds one's basic confidence. At that center, one fears or makes one's peace with death. Here is the ultimate privacy where one comes ultimately to face the reality of God—though that name may not be used. But to the degree to which one faces one's own mortality and determines whether one can trust, one is facing the question of one's relationship to God. The pastor discovers that everyone has that core of personhood, and the basic questions are the same for us all. The distinctions that mark persons drop away before the imperious demands of selfhood. The president of the company has to come to terms with the core of personhood as well as the humblest member of the organization.

Albert Camus once spoke of the writer's life as "the long journeying to recover . . . the two or three simple and great images which first gained access to his heart."[2] So with every person, while no one else can fully enter into that search, there are occasions when the minister is invited to share a surprising intimacy in other people's lives.

Yet, this admission is granted to one *as a pastor,* not merely as a person. This interpretation may be open to debate, but in the main I believe it to be true. Thus ministers' relationships are a paradox. They know an unusual number of people whom they can call by name. Their circle of acquaintances is large, but these relationships are on a fairly superficial level. On the other hand, ministers have the kind of relationships of which we have been speaking, where they have been admitted as ministers to the primary experiences of others' lives. Yet it sometimes seems that ministers have a minimum of relationships between these two extremes! The minister's spouse may feel this most poignantly.

Many things contribute to this situation. Most people want to present only their best side to their minister! They often project on him or her attitudes which are carried over from the minister they knew as children. They even impute a judgmental attitude which is not actually held by the minister! They will not give the pastor a chance to cease being a minister for a while, and become a person in one's own right.

In short, it often takes more time than usual to establish relationships which go below the surface to a real friendship where one is accepted for oneself. In the contemporary scene this is changing, but it still is true that some have felt a loneliness in the ministry, a loneliness which seems strange when they are surrounded by people.

WORK

Sooner or later someone asks us about the ministry, "Just what is it that you do?" It sometimes is embarrassing to try to answer that! It all sounds so vague, indefinite, and unprofessional! A little of this and a little of that! But when one steps back a little and looks at the minister's work, it may be clear that certain characteristics which on occasion prove troublesome are, in fact, its strength and its appeal.

Manysidedness

Sometimes it seems impossible to be as versatile as the ministry requires. There is the preaching, in itself a definite skill. But there also is administration, the organizing of the life of the congregation to provide a particular kind of fellowship and do a particular kind of work. There is also ministry to individuals, as we have already noted, as counselor and pastor. And there is always something to be promoted, for we are part of a larger structure of our denomination which is seeking to carry out a mission for all the churches. Then, of course, we have responsibilities within the community. On the surface the task *does* seem impossible.

The hope, of course, is to enlist a wide group of lay people to share in the ministry. Yet, this strategy is not as much a time-saver, for the enlistment itself is time-demanding, as an enrichment of ministry.

Two things make this manysidedness possible. One is the awareness that all these elements are facets of the same ministry to people, "varieties of service but the same Lord." There is a meaning which makes the diversity hold together. These various functions can support one another. They can be an enrichment rather than a conflict.

The other truth is that this very alternation makes the work of the minister attractive to some. It is an interesting moment when the door of the study closes and one has some time to seek understanding. But it is also an interesting moment when it opens again and the pastor goes out to be with people and bring that understanding to bear upon human need. That coming in and the going out enrich each other. To find this alternation appealing is probably one of the qualifications for the pastorate of a local church.

Time

In a day when many have their priorities of time and energy set by others, the minister still has some free choices. No one tells the pastor how to divide his or her time. For some, this freedom is more than they can handle creatively! The result is disorder and an ad hoc existence. Moreover, it would be foolish to imply that we have complete control over our time. Far from it. John Frederick Oberlin was a man whose creative ministry for half a century in the Valley of Stone in the Vosges Mountains left an enduring mark on Christian ministry. Yet he could complain:

> The pastor at Waldsbach, if he tries to be what he ought to be in this vast and most burdensome parish which does not at all resemble those of the plain, is a poor dog, a beast of burden, a cart-horse. He must do everything, watch everything, provide for everything, answer for everything. From early morning until bed-time I am occupied, hurried, crushed, without being able to do half or the tenth part of what ought to be done. A decent leisure, which others can enjoy, has long been unknown to me. . . . Who cares? Everything rests upon the pastor, who meets everywhere nothing but hindrances, obstacles, delays and red tape; and, not being able to please everybody, or satisfy those who disagree with each other, must fight constantly against malevolence.[3]

We often know the feeling! But it still is true that to a notable degree pastors have sufficient freedom to set some priorities and determine what has first claim on their time. This should not be oversimplified, for there are many occasions when one has to do what needs to be done even though it is not first choice. But compared to others in the contemporary scene, the minister has opportunity to be self-directed and autonomous—so much so that if the pastor does not determine priorities, no one else will do it!

The failure to set some priorities for ourselves leaves us open to that bane of the ministry—trivia. The time WILL fill up. Trivia rush in where angels fail to tread! They take over the agenda at board and committee meetings. They fill our days, giving us the illusion of being busy and really keeping us from facing the main business of our ministry. They make pastoral calls a game we play instead of human encounter. Most of all, they deprive the ministry of its real satisfactions, leaving us restless and unfulfilled. While all human endeavor is subject to triviality, the ministry seems particularly susceptible, especially when the minister fails to exercise the prerogative to set his or her own priorities.

Incompletion

One of the satisfactions often denied ministers is seeing the precise results of our work. We deal with the incomplete and the imprecise. Much of what we do must be marked "unfinished business." We can see an episode through to its immediate end, but the final outcome often remains hidden and unknown. How often we wonder how it came out! We have to do the one thing possible, perhaps no more than being with the person in need for a little while.

This sense of incompleteness marks a lifetime of ministry. Many will understand what Oliver Wendell Holmes said of his own life, when on his fifty-ninth birthday he ended his time on the Supreme Judicial Court of Massachusetts:

> I ask myself, what is to show for this half lifetime that has passed? I look into my book in which I keep a docket of the decisions of the full court which fall to me to write, and find about a thousand cases . . . many of them upon trifling or transitory matters, to represent nearly half a lifetime. . . .

> Alas, gentlemen, that is life. . . . We cannot live our dreams. We are lucky enough if we can give a sample of our best, and if in our hearts we can feel it has been nobly done.[4]

In some ways the prototype of the ministry is Moses at Mount Nebo, allowed to see the Promised Land but not to enter in! Yet who can doubt that in his heart Moses long had possessed the Promised Land even in the midst of the wilderness? The writer of Hebrews summarized the experience poignantly, "All these died in faith, not having received what was promised . . ." (Hebrews 11:13), but adds, "God had foreseen something better . . ." (Hebrews 11:40). The first is the fact, the latter the faith which marks the ministry with its inevitable incompletion.

STUDY

Can one carry scholarly interests into the pastorate of a local church? Aren't pastoral concerns more "practical," making real scholarship really impossible and even undesirable as "too academic"? Is the term "scholarly pastor" a contradiction?

To be sure, there is a kind of scholarship which suggests that the scholar and the pastor will not be interested in each other. That scholarship is clearly meant for an academic setting which would provide a setting congenial to research and specialization.

But there also is a scholarship appropriate to the pastorate. In fact, the combination of study on the one hand and participation in the life of the congregation on the other is the ideal setting for deepening the understanding of the Christian faith. More recently we have used the terms "action" and "reflection" as a process of learning, but that has been the scholarship of the pastorate for a long time. The life within the parish and the hours in the study illumine each other. Here are seen guilt and forgiveness, sin and salvation, lostness and redemption, judgment and grace. What an understanding there is in letting the study give insight into the parish, and the parish provide the study with the data of human existence!

It cannot be said too strongly that congregational life was the seedbed of the great Christian doctrines—and it still is. It was not in a discussion group that such doctrines were born. Nor was it "in the world." It was in congregational life, and humble congregational life, at that. Imagine the Corinthian church as the setting for learning the meaning of agape love! Or Rome as the setting for understanding grace! Here in struggling little congregations Christians hammered out the meaning of the forgiveness, obedience, grace, and saviorhood which had come to them in Jesus Christ. And ever since, these majestic concepts have been given new meaning, nurtured in the life of the congregation.

The pastorate is indeed a superb setting for living scholarship. The pastorate will not *make* one a scholar. No setting will. But it will *allow* it. More than that, it will feed the scholarly interest even when it cannot create that interest. And to the one who carries that interest as part of the vocation, the pastorate provides a lifelong stimulus and immense satisfactions.

FAMILY RELATIONS

A number of factors have served to break the stereotype of the minister's family. As is true of most stereotypes, it often did not conform to reality—the wife as an unnamed and unpaid assistant minister and the children as automatic leaders of the youth group! Many a church assumed that in calling the minister they were getting a package deal! Though this stereotype never was really true, now we *know* it isn't! And we're better for it.

What is being affirmed here in relation to the minister's family is a basic right, namely, the right to choose. The wife or husband of the minister may choose to share in the ministry of the spouse. If so, he or she may find in it a real fulfillment. In this the ministry is distinctive in our culture, for the average person cannot share in the work of his or her spouse. So, many in the pastor's family will choose to do so. But the sharing has to be voluntary, not imposed.

Equally, the spouse may choose *not* to do so, and that decision must be respected. It does not necessarily reflect a lack of interest in the church or its mission. The decision may be to pursue one's own calling, or no calling, like any other member of the church. After all, a spouse marries a person who is a minister, not the ministry itself!

Increasingly, economic necessity has made it necessary for many wives to seek work outside the home to supplement the family income, especially at times when there is unusual expense, as in the college years.

Equally, the children of the minister have their personal rights, and most of us have discovered that they have a way of asserting them! Like any family, there are years, when the children are young, when decisions about participation in the life of the church are made as a family. But the time comes—sooner than we expect—when the decision has to be made individually. That is a basic right—and need—of all children, including the minister's.

In my first year in college I came home full of new and strange ideas. After trying them out one night on my father, I became aware of something I had not seen before. He had never told me what I *should* believe. When I pointed out my discovery to him, he said, "Well, we made a decision about that a long time ago. We decided that we would not tell our sons what they had to believe. But we would try to show them that what we believe is important." Though our beliefs often differed, we always had common ground.

Another right, of course, is the decision not to marry. Singleness is a legitimate life-style for some, and the decision is a personal one. To advocate marriage because it is "required" by the nature of the pastorate is to put life's most basic human relationship on a false foundation.

When by their own choice the pastor's family members enter into the work of the church, their participation can prove a source of immense satisfaction. The church becomes an extended family in which is found a surprising measure of love and affection. With a little humor and much grace the relationship can be cherished by both church and family. The interest in the minister's children becomes not intrusive but supportive. Most of us who grew up in preacher's homes remember our extended family with real appreciation.

PERSONAL FAITH

Who will be pastor to the pastor? This is a question often asked but rarely answered. Increasingly attempts are being made to provide, in denominational structures, supervisory pastors, and they are of help. But there are times in a minister's life when the need is personal and not official.

By the nature of ministry, there are supports to faith which others may not see. The closer we are to human experience the more we can speak of "that which we have seen and heard." As has been said a number of times on these pages, God's greatest disclosures are in human experience. Here one sees faith at work.

When I was a student in theological school, I spent a weekend with friends at a lakeside home where Dr. Justin Wroe Nixon, a distinguished teacher and preacher, was also a guest. Because he was suffering from laryngitis, Dr. Nixon had to carry on conversation by writing on a pad! In this interesting way we began to talk about theology, particularly as it related to pastoral experience, for I had just started in a village church.

At one point Dr. Nixon wrote on his pad the question "How do you think of Jesus?" Then he listed some alternatives: "As a social prophet? As a teacher? As God?" I said that my whole feeling about Jesus had taken on new dimensions since I began my pastoral responsibilities. When I visited a hospital, I thought of Jesus' healing. When I sat with a troubled person, I remembered how he reached out and brought calm. Where there was bereavement, I remembered his times of comforting. In short, he had become far more real as I faced actual human situations. Jesus Christ was somehow present to us. At this, Dr. Nixon took his pencil and on his pad checked, "As God."

Now, a lifetime of ministry later, that conviction is stronger than ever. The pastorate has been my teacher. Deeper than that, it has been a source of disclosure again and again. I understand Jesus Christ because I have seen the human condition to which he came "to seek and save that which is lost." In this way, pastoral experience supports, enhances, and deepens personal faith.

Yet the greatest disclosure of the meaning of faith in God comes at the very point of greatest difficulty—human suffering. Sometimes its weight is almost more than we can bear.

Recently I came away from a hospital where a beautiful young woman was dying. At the hospital door I had to step back to let a young man go by, led by the hand in his blindness. That moment is still vivid, for the awful reality of human suffering suddenly broke in upon me. I stood on the sidewalk in rebellion and pain at the injustice of it.

But the paradox is that just when the weight of human suffering is most grievous, when we would least expect God's nearness, there comes the deep-down conviction that God, in Christ, stands with us. One understands what we mean when we speak of God's suffering in the world. He shares in it. The pastorate teaches us that truth, if we will give it time. So faith is deepened, not because we have thought it through, but because we have lived it through. We have seen people say,

> "When other helpers fail, and comforts flee,
> Help of the helpless, O abide with me."

And He does.

Yet the pastor will experience all the fluctuations of faith— sometimes more than others. We are supposed to be men and women of faith, and yet at times our faith simply recedes. Or it gives us days that are dull and spiritless. Or often, to the anguish of unfaith is added the burden of guilt. *We* ought not lose faith! But we learn to wait it out as we sometimes wait for the coming of morning, trusting the little faith that we have and doubting our unfaith. Some of us have found the time of unfaith shortened because, crisis or not, faith was required of us—to give to someone else. So we offered the fragment we had at the time and it somehow proved adequate, feeding not five thousand, but at least feeding!

Early in the sixteenth century, Hugh Latimer preached a memorable sermon in King's Chapel, Cambridge. It was impressive in its intellectual scope and its eloquence. As the sermon was finished and Latimer came down from the high pulpit, he was met at the foot of the stairs by one of the clergy, known as Little Bilney. "Prithee,

Father Latimer, may I confess my soul to thee?" said Bilney. So they went into an adjoining room, and there Bilney poured out his anguish and his need. As Bilney spoke, Latimer's eyes filled with tears and he confessed that he, too, knew the same anguish. So they prayed together not only for themselves but also for the state of the church in England.[5] In that moment was a beginning of the enlightenment, a time of freshening which made its impact on all of England.

Can it be that, in the times when our personal faith seems taken away, God is but making room for his next gifts? He is clearing the field for a fresh planting.

ACCEPTING THE CALL

The matters which have been our concern in these pages come to their focus in the call to a pastorate. What does the authentic pastor say in response? What will be his or her manner of life in that congregation? What covenant will the pastor keep? It can be caught up in words of commitment:

As your preacher, to bring week by week to the fullest of my ability, a disciplined and authentic word of the gospel as it must be understood and trusted in our time.

As your pastor, to be faithful in pastoral care, to be with you in times of need and decision, in times of celebration and thanksgiving; to respect every word confided in me as a trust never to be violated.

As your minister, to administer the affairs of the church responsibly; to find new ways for new days; to call on others and to do nothing I can get someone else to do better!

As one committed to the church, to join with you in keeping the Christian institution related to this time of revolution and renewal.

As a Christian citizen, to seek to live responsibly in this community and to be active in those decisions that affect our common life.

As a Christian person, to enjoy these years remembering that our faith is essentially a joyous and victorious way of life letting us take high pleasure in the privilege of being human together.

As a servant of Christ, to remember that of all the gifts in the church, as the Apostle said, the greatest is love.

In this sense, and trusting in God's grace, I accept your call.

Notes

INTRODUCTION

[1] Frederick W. Robertson, Preface by C. B. Robertson, *Sermons by the Rev. Frederick W. Robertson, M.A.* (London: Kegan Paul, Trench, Trubner, and Co., Ltd., 1907), pp. xiv-xv.

CHAPTER 1

[1] Thomas Merton, *Seven Storey Mountain* (New York: Harcourt Brace Jovanovich, Inc., 1948), p. 176.

[2] Studs Terkel, *Working* (New York: Pantheon Books, 1974), p. xi.

[3] T. S. Eliot, *The Complete Poems and Plays, 1909-1950* (New York: Harcourt Brace Jovanovich, Inc., 1952), p. 362.

[4] William James, *The Varieties of Religious Experience* (New York: Modern Library, 1902), pp. 498-499.

CHAPTER 2

[1] Alexander V. G. Allen, *Life and Letters of Phillips Brooks*, vol. 1 (New York: E. P. Dutton and Co., 1901), pp. 264-265.

[2] Gabriel Fackre, *Humiliation and Celebration* (New York: Sheed and Ward, Inc., 1969), p. 35.

[3] Alvin Toffler, *Future Shock* (New York: Random House, Inc., 1970), pp. 71-72.

[4] Elizabeth Nowell, *Thomas Wolfe, a Biography* (Garden City, N.Y.: Doubleday & Co., Inc., 1960), p. 184.

CHAPTER 3

[1] Jimmy Breslin, *How the Good Guys Finally Won* (New York: The Viking Press, 1975), p. 53.

CHAPTER 4

[1] D. Macmillan, *Life of George Matheson* (New York: A. C. Armstrong & Son, 1907), pp. 325-326.

CHAPTER 5

[1] William James, *The Varieties of Religious Experience* (New York: The Modern Library, 1902), p. 186.

[2] Ernest Mortimer, *Blaise Pascal, The Life and Work of a Realist* (London: Methuen & Co Ltd., 1959), p. 120.

[3] Will Herberg, *Four Existentialist Theologians* (Garden City, N.Y.: Doubleday & Co., Anchor Books, 1958), p. 163.

[4] William James, *The Letters of William James*, vol. 1 (Boston: Atlantic Monthly Press, 1920), p. 148.

[5] *Ibid.*, p. 169.

[6] *Ibid.*, p. 147.

[7] Dorothy Berkley Phillips, ed., *The Choice Is Always Ours* (New York: Harper & Row, Publishers, 1960), p. 67.

CHAPTER 6

[1] William Cullen Bryant, "The Crowded Street," *Poetical Works of William Cullen Bryant* (New York: D. Appleton and Company, 1901), p. 208.

[2] Alan Paton, "Meditation for a Young Boy Confirmed," *Christian Century*, vol. 71, no. 41 (October 13, 1954), p. 1239. Used with permission of Charles Scribner's Sons.

CHAPTER 7

[1] Brendan Behan, *The Quare Fellow and the Hostage* (New York: Grove Press, Inc., 1964), pp. 95-96.

[2] Pitirim A. Sorokin, *The Crisis of Our Age* (New York: E. P. Dutton & Co., Inc., 1941), p. 22.

[3] Charles Howard Hopkins, *The Rise of the Social Gospel in American Protestantism* (New Haven: Yale University Press, 1940), p. 8.

[4] Shailer Mathews and G. B. Smith, *A Dictionary of Religion and Ethics* (New York: The Macmillan Company, 1921), pp. 416-417.

[5] Dietrich Bonhoeffer, *Letters and Papers from Prison* (New York: The Macmillan Company, 1971), pp. 16-17.

CHAPTER 8

[1] Willard L. Sperry, *Reality in Worship* (New York: The Macmillan Company, 1952), p. 168.

[2] Walter Rauschenbusch, "In the Presence of God," *Golden Book of Religious Verse,* compiled by Thomas Curtis Clark (Garden City, N.Y.: Garden City Publishing Company, Inc., n.d.), p. 4.

[3] P. T. Forsyth, *Positive Preaching and the Modern Mind* (New York: A. C. Armstrong & Son, 1907), p. 5.

[4] In *Colgate Rochester Divinity School Bulletin,* vol. 36, no. 6 (June, 1964), p. 44.

[5] John E. Skoglund, *A Manual of Worship* (Valley Forge: Judson Press, 1968).

CHAPTER 9

[1] Quoted in Gordon W. Allport, *Personality, a Psychological Interpretation* (New York: Henry Holt & Co., 1937), p. 213.

[2] Germaine Brée, *Camus* (New Brunswick, N.J.: Rutgers University Press, 1961), p. 63.

[3] Marshall Dawson, *Oberlin, a Protestant Saint* (Chicago: Willett, Clark & Company, 1934), p. 109.

[4] Dean Acheson, *Present at the Creation* (New York: W. W. Norton & Co., Inc., 1969), p. 725.

[5] F. W. Boreham, *A Bunch of Everlastings* (Nashville: Abingdon Press, 1920), pp. 56-59.